Here's What People
Inspiration For Stu

"Inspiration is the key to success. This book will give ... y leader who may be feeling frustrated, discouraged or fatigued the inspiration to re-energize themselves and their fellow peers!"
Christopher Zisko, Student Leader at Monmouth University & NACA Board of Directors Student Representative

"This volume will provide encouragement to many young would-be leaders who might otherwise hesitate to take the risks that leadership entails. Bravo to the book's contributors for sharing their experience and know-how!"
Dr. Leslie J. Delauter, House Dean, University of Pennsylvania

"After reading the stories from this book I felt overcome with inspiration. Great Job!"
Theresa Ann Sadler, Graduate Student in Higher Education, Rowan University

"This book helps student leaders to understand the frustrations and successes which they share with their peers across the country."
Emily Sama Martin, Student Leader at University of Pennsylvania

"This book is not only an inspiration, but a collection of thought provoking writings that will enrich and challenge the leader in all of us!"
Chuck Simpson, Associate Director of Campus Activities, SUNY Upstate Medical University

"No matter whether you're a student or a professional this is just what the doctor ordered to reenergize the spirit of any leader."
Larry Mannolini, Assistant Director of Campus Life, Alfred University

"There's no better way to find a 'kick of inspiration' than from the stories of your peers. These are the people who've already stood where you are now, and have made it through successfully!"
Pamela Chimino, Assistant Director of Student Activities
Genesee Community College

"This book is an awesome and encouraging book. So many times, I feel that I am the only one trying to change the things I don't like by being whole-heartedly involved. This book helps me to remember that I am not the only one seeking to better America. I recommend it to anyone seeking to better himself or herself and to help those around them do the same."
Katie S. Bailes, Student Leader at Shawnee State University

"Lead, Follow and Read this Book! Inspiration for Student Leaders is a testament to every student leader who dared to go beyond the classroom—learning to acknowledge his/her spirit, face challenges of diversity, and embrace one's own life. Truly, this book is call to action to cease the moment and lead for a lifetime."
Shane Windmeyer, Coordinator Lambda 10 Project for GLBT Issues

"Inspiration for Student Leaders is an enlightening and insightful collection of narratives that provides readers with a meaningful look at the college experience of those who dare to lead."
Seamus McManus, Residential Living Marketing Coordinator
Drexel University

"The challenges that face our world today necessitate that we nurture individuals with commitment, energy, and intelligence who are able to translate these traits into proactive ideas and solutions. Inspiration for Student Leaders will not only inspire student leaders to develop such ideas and solutions; It will inspire them take action!"
Cliff Scutella, Director of Student Activities,
Genesee Community College

Inspiration™
FOR STUDENT LEADERS

ENCOURAGEMENT

HUMOR & MOTIVATION

FOR

STUDENT LEADERS

BY

STUDENT LEADERS

The Collegiate
EmPowerment Company, Inc.
www.Collegiate-EmPowerment.com
Toll Free: 1.877.338.8246

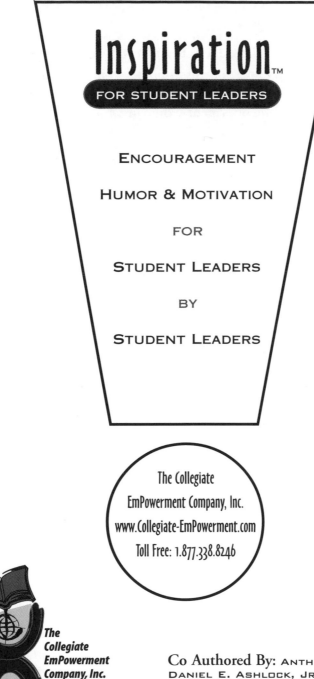

The
Collegiate
EmPowerment
Company, Inc.

"The Leader in EmPowerment Education for Today's College Students"

Co Authored By: ANTHONY J. D'ANGELO, DANIEL E. ASHLOCK, JR., LUCY SHAFFER CROFT, DAN OLTERSDORF, W.H. "BUTCH" OXENDINE, MARY ALICE OZECHOSKI AND ELIZABETH RANDAZZESE

Copyright © 2002 The Collegiate EmPowerment Company, Inc.
All rights reserved. No part of this publication may be reproduced in
any form without written permission from The Collegiate
EmPowerment Company, Inc.
For permission please call toll free 1.877.338.8246
We will be happy to help you.

Published by:

The
Collegiate
EmPowerment
Company, Inc.

"Helping You Take Higher Education Deeper™"

EASTON, PA 18040
WWW.COLLEGIATE-EMPOWERMENT.COM

2003 Second Print Edition
Printed with Pride in The United States Of America
ISBN: 0-9646957-3-1

BOOKS ARE AVAILABLE IN QUANTITY DISCOUNTS WHEN USED
FOR STUDENT LEADER DEVELOPMENT AND RECOGNITION.
FOR PRICING INFORMATION PLEASE SEE THE LAST PAGE AT
THE BACK OF THIS BOOK. THANK YOU.

*We would like to thank all the contributing authors for
permission to reprint their submissions. Please refer to
the back of this book for individual acknowledgements.*

The Inspiration Book Series

This Book is
Dedicated to You,
The Student Leader

Inspiration for Student leaders

Table of Contents

Introduction *by Anthony J. D'Angelo* 9

About The Authors 11

Acknowledgements 14

Charitable Partner Highlight Page: NACA 15

Start With Yourself *by Anonymous* 16

What Every College Creed Ought To Be
by Anthony J. D'Angelo 17

Do It Anyway *by Elizabeth Randazzese* 18

To Be A Leader *Author Unknown* 21

True Leaders Never Lose *by David Tukey* 22

Just Belong *Author Unknown* 24

The Day I Was A Dipstick *by Anthony J. D'Angelo* 25

The Quandary of Jewels *by Daniel E. Ashlock* 29

Getting An Education, Not Just A Degree
by Anthony J. D'Angelo 32

These Are The Days
Author Unknown, Submitted by Debra Lamp 34

Discover Your Own Acre of Diamonds
by Russell Conwell 37

Women Who Dare & Who Helped Us All
by Anthony J. D'Angelo 41

The Sense of A Goose *Author Unknown* 44

Are You Strong Enough To Handle The Critics?
by Theodore Roosevelt 46

Complications *by Mark Walker* *47*

The Purpose of Student Leaders *by Elizabeth Randazzese* . . .*50*

The Chopsticks of Heaven & Hell *by Anthony J. D'Angelo* . .*52*

Lessons From a Fly *by Dan Oltersdorf* *53*

Just Because It's Tradition, Doesn't Make It Right
by Anthony J. D'Angelo *59*

Leadership Demonstrated By Picking Up Trash
by George Brelsford *60*

A Memo To Student Leaders *by The Boss* *62*

How To Get An A On Your Final Exam
by Anthony J. D'Angelo *65*

Pebbles In Your Pockets *by Thomas W. Smith* *68*

When In Doubt Do What Gandhi Would Do
Author Unknown *69*

The Secret to Leadership *by Elizabeth Randazzese* *70*

What Legacy Will You Leave? *by Anthony J. D'Angelo* *72*

What Is A Leader? *by Stephen M. Vindigni* *74*

Success *by Ralph Waldo Emerson* *76*

A Simple Lesson About Leadership
by Anthony J. D'Angelo *77*

Seeking To Understand *by Brian Dassler* *79*

If You Talk The Talk, You Better Walk The Walk
by Anthony J. D'Angelo 83*

Leadership Is About Perspective, Not Position
by Frank Koch *84*

What Being A Student Leader Is All About
by Anthony J. D'Angelo *86*

The Sermons We See *by Edgar A. Guest* 88

Politics Is Doing The Popular Thing, Leadership Is Doing
The Right Thing *by a Student Leader* 89

The Golden Rules For Living & Leadership
Author Unknown 92

There Are Professors and Then There Are Educators
by Anthony J. D'Angelo 93

The Animal School *by Dr. R.H. Reeves* 94

The Orientation Leader *by Meghan Greene* 96

The Parable of The Chinese Bamboo Tree
by Anthony J. D'Angelo 97

Lessons From The Playground *by Dan Ashlock* 98

Onward and Upward *by Lucy Croft* 102

The Chipped Tea Cup *by Anthony J. D'Angelo* 105

The Boy Under The Tree
by David Coleman and Kevin Randall *106*

We Want Your Story for Volume II *111*

Permissions *112*

The Collegiate EmPowerment Company Story *114*

An Overview of
The Collegiate EmPowerment Company *116*

What College Forgets To Teach You® Seminar Series *118*

The Student Leader Strategic Advantage™ Overview .*122*

Ordering Information *124*

Welcome To The Inspiration Book Series!

Dear Student Leader,
Thank you for reading *Inspiration for Student Leaders*. The book you are holding has been made possible by people just like you. This book, as well as the entire Inspiration Book Series, is a compilation of stories of encouragement, humor and motivation by college students for college students. Simply put, this book is for YOU and by YOU.

This whole "Inspiration Revolution" was started by two college students, Dan Oltersdorf and Amy Connolly, the co-authors of *Inspiration for Resident Assistants*. The vision which we had back in 1999 has now manifested itself into a seven part book series. This is number three in the series and we've got four more on the way.

From the outset, our intention was never to create a New York Times Bestseller. Rather it has been our vision to create a vehicle for college students to inspire each other with their own story. After all, every person has a story to share.

The word Inspiration means "In Spirit". As student leaders we know that student leadership is not about holding a position. It is about having a passion. It is about serving our campus community In Spirit. It may be a Spirit of pride, a Spirit of commitment or a Spirit of love. No matter what Spirit you lead with, one thing holds true. The Spirit which you bring to the world is yours and yours to share with others.

The world needs your Spirit now more than ever. You see the sad reality is that most people are not getting what they want. Not from their education, not from their professors, not from their jobs, not from their families, not from their religion, not from their government, not from one another and most importantly, not from themselves. Something is missing in most of our lives. What most people need is a place of community that has higher purpose and deeper meaning. A place which being human is a prerequisite, but acting human is essential. A place that replaces the home that many of us have seemingly lost.

That is what your student organization can become. It can become a place of community. If can become a place where words such as integrity, concern, compassion, vision and excellence can be used not as nouns, but as action verbs. The kind of place that gives people a sense that your organization is a special place, created by special people doing what they do in the best possible way. And all being done for the simplest, most human reason possible, because they are alive! What other reason do you need?

We human beings are capable of performing extraordinary acts. Capable of going to the moon. Capable of bottling powdered tea mix and then selling it for 100 times the cost of making it. Capable of creating computers. Capable of creating killer equations like $e=mc^2$. Capable of making Tupperware lids that actually fit. Capable of flying planes filled with people into our national symbols.

The least we should be able to do is create a sense of community on our campus. A sense of caring. Caring for our school. Caring for our organization. Caring for ourselves and most of all, caring for one another.

On behalf of the entire *Inspiration for Student Leaders* team, I want to thank you for reading our book. We hope you enjoy it and become inspired to share your own story with us.

To Your Success!
Anthony J. D'Angelo, Creator of The Inspiration Book Series™

PS- Drop me an email: Anthony@Collegiate-EmPowerment.com
I like hearing from our readers & student leaders like you!

About The Authors:

Anthony J. D'Angelo, The Collegiate EmPowerment Coach™,  is a graduate of West Chester University of PA where he served as president of the student government association. Anthony is the founder of The Collegiate EmPowerment Company, Inc. (CEC) and the creator of The Inspiration Book Series™. Since 1995, he and the CEC team have served over 1 Million college students from over 1,500 schools across North America, Europe & Australia. He has a loving relationship with his wife Christine and enjoys kayaking & the beach.

Daniel E. Ashlock Jr. is currently the Director of Student  Activities at Towson University (MD). Daniel is a graduate of Northern Arizona University and Central Connecticut State University. He has been a student affairs professional for more than 10 years having also worked at Pittsburg State University (KS) and Lycoming College (PA). Daniel has been a volunteer for the National Association for Campus Activities (NACA) since 1988 in a variety of regional and national positions. He has written numerous articles for Campus Activities Programming magazine. Daniel was named the Outstanding Campus Activities Professional by the NACA East Coast Region in 1998 and the Outstanding New Campus Activities Professional by the NACA Heart of America Region in 1994. He is happily married to Renee and is very proud of their children, Nathan and Quinlyn.

Lucy Shaffer Croft is currently the Director of Student Organizations & Activities at the University of Cincinnati. Lucy received her undergraduate degree from Hanover College, IN and her Master's from the University of Cincinnati in Ohio. She began her Student Affairs profession at Pratt Institute in Brooklyn, New York and has worked as the Director of Student Activities at Virginia Intermont College in Bristol, Virginia. Lucy has been affiliated with the National Association for Campus Activities (NACA) since 1987. Over the past fourteen years, she has presented educational sessions at a local, regional and national level. She has been selected as the 2003 National Convention Chair in Nashville, TN. Lucy is currently completing her Doctorate in Education. When she is not studying or educating she enjoys playing tennis & being married .

Dan Oltersdorf is the founder of the internationally known residence life resource website ResidentAssistant.com, and is a co-author of *Inspiration for Resident Assistants.* He has been involved in numerous areas of student leadership during his undergraduate experience at Colorado State University, in the Higher Education master's program at Florida State University. Through his speaking, writing, and online resources, Dan works with student leaders all over the world to prepare and position them for success.

W.H. "Butch" Oxendine, Jr. is president of Oxendine

Publishing, Inc. and for 19 years has been editor in chief of *Student Leader* and *Florida Leader* magazines. He is the author of *Poster Secrets: How & Where to Hang Flyers on Your Campus* and *So You Want to Be President... How to Get Elected on Your Campus.* Butch has been published in more than 200 publications nationwide and is a frequent presenter at leadership conventions.

Mary-Alice Ozechoski has been involved in student life for over 15 years. She currently works at Teikyo Post University as the Associate Vice President of Student Life. Mary-Alice has served on numerous committees, conferences and conventions of the National Association for Campus Activities. She is also an active member of the National Association of Student Personnel Administrators. In addition Mary-Alice has done leadership training across the Northeast.

Elizabeth Randazzese has been committed to student leadership

since her undergraduate years at Rowan University, where she served as President of The Student Government Association. Currently she is completing her graduate work at the University of Pennsylvania's School of Social Work. In addition to her studies, Elizabeth is a Certified Collegiate EmPowerment Coach™ with The Collegiate EmPowerment Company, Inc. and a member of the EmPower X! Team. Elizabeth has the distinction of being the first female to join the EmPower X! Team.

Acknowledgements and Appreciation

This project would not be possible without the support, guidance and inspiration of the following individuals. We are very, very grateful for you.

Pamela Moss, SEA & Associate Editor of The Inspiration Book Series™. Without you none of this would be possible. Your ability to create team synergy is your gift to the world.

Taralynn Ross, of Browndog Design, the Goddess of Graphic Design. Thanks for bringing life to the Vision once again. Your ability to visually package emotions is your brilliance.

Alan Davis, Executive Director of NACA. Thank you for your Faith in this project. Here's to our success!

The Angels of Whizzer Bike Investments. Thank you for making me accept the 1984 Manor Elementary School Best Story Teller Award. Don't worry I'll remember to "Watch out for the Whizzer Bikes."

Our families, friends and colleagues who gave us the love and support we needed to make this book a reality.

Mark Victor Hansen, the co-creator of *Chicken Soup For The Soul*®. Thank you for teaching us all how to THINK BIG. You are a cherished mentor and a dear friend. It is an honor to have been taken under your wing. I will make you proud, I promise.

Dan Sullivan, The Strategic Coach®. Thank you for transforming the educational system of America from the inside-out. Your brilliance is light years ahead of the old school bureaucrats. On behalf of my grandchildren, thank you for what your work has done and will do for this world. I'm in it for the long haul too.

Our Clients & Students. The Collegiate EmPowerment Company is a reflection of all that we have learned from you. You are our greatest gift. Thank you for allowing us to help you take higher education deeper. It has been an honor to serve you. Here's to our continued partnership and success!

Supporting The People Who Support Student Leaders

In the spirit of empowering today's college students,
The Collegiate EmPowerment Company, Inc., recognizes,
The National Association for Campus Activities (NACA) as the
Charitable Benefactor of Inspiration for Student Leaders™.
The Collegiate EmPowerment Company will donate One Dollar
from every book sold to NACA. This money will help support
NACA as it pursues its Vision and Mission.

Founded in 1960, The National Association For Campus Activities
(NACA) is the nation's largest not-for-profit college organization for
campus activities, with programs and services designed to reflect the
field's increasing responsibilities for student leadership and development, as well as entertainment programming.

NACA membership is composed of colleges and universities, talent
firms and artist/performers, student programmers and leaders, and
professional campus activities staff. NACA's activities and services
inspire excellence in student leadership development outside the college
classroom, linking the higher education and entertainment communities
and also providing a unique forum for business and professional
development, information exchange and networking.

National Association for Campus Activities
13 Harbison Way • Columbia, South Carolina 29212-3401
Phone: 803.732.6222 • www.naca.org

naca

Start With Yourself
By Anonymous

The following words are written on the tomb of an Anglican bishop in the crypts of Westminster Abbey:

When I was young and free and my imagination had no limits, I dreamed of changing the world. As I grew older and wiser, I discovered the world would not change, so I shortened my sights somewhat and decided to change only my country.

But it too seemed immovable.

As I grew into my twilight years, in one last desperate attempt, I settled for changing only my family, those closest to me, but alas, they would have none of it.

And now as I lay on my deathbed, I suddenly realize: If I had only changed myself first, then by example, I would have changed my family.

From their inspiration and encouragement, I would then have been able to better my country and, who knows, I may have even changed the world. ★

What Every College Creed Ought To Be
By Anthony J. D'Angelo

STUDENTS are...
Important people on this campus.

Not cold enrollment statistics, but flesh & blood,
human beings with feelings & emotions like our own.

Not people to be tolerated
so that we can do our own thing.

THEY ARE OUR THING.

Not dependent on us.
Rather we are both interdependent upon one another.
Not an interruption of our work,
but the purpose of it.

Without students there would
be no need for this institution. ★

Do It Anyway!
By Elizabeth Randazzese

Many amazing leaders have come before us to show us the meaning of leadership. Some of these men and women have left us volumes of written works giving us insight about leadership, and their words continue to inspire us. But one of the greatest leaders of all time, Mother Teresa, led through action as well as through words. We know many things about this amazing woman. She won the Noble Peace Prize in 1979, she founded a new religious order and she established schools and food centers for the destitute. Most of us can still remember these actions and their impact on the people she helped.

Hanging on the wall of one of the children's homes she founded, there is a sign that shares the following words about the actions we should take:

Sometimes, people are
unreasonable, illogical, and self-centered.
LOVE THEM ANYWAY.

Often, if you do good, people
will accuse you of selfish, ulterior motives.
DO GOOD ANYWAY.

There is a risk that if you are successful,
you will win false friends and true enemies.
SUCCEED ANYWAY.

There is always the possibility that the good
 you do today will be forgotten tomorrow.
DO GOOD ANYWAY.

People will remind you that honesty
and frankness make you vulnerable.
BE HONEST AND FRANK ANYWAY.

There is a chance that what you spend
years building may be destroyed overnight.
BUILD ANYWAY.

If you find serenity and
happiness, they may be jealous.
BE HAPPY ANYWAY.

Give the world the best that you have,
 and it may never be enough.
GIVE THE WORLD THE BEST YOU'VE GOT ANYWAY.

To the student leaders that have come and gone from college;
remember these powerful words for all your life. As long as you
are alive, you will be leading someone or something. So,
remember Mother Teresa's words: Do it anyway, for the mere
fact that it is the right thing to do. ★

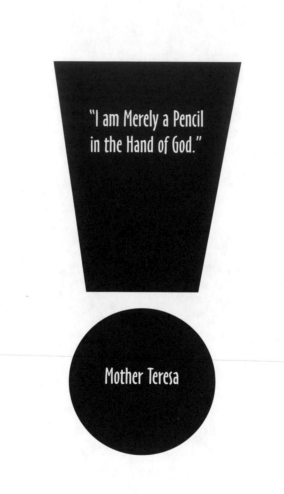

"I am Merely a Pencil
in the Hand of God."

Mother Teresa

To Be A Leader
Author Unknown

You must endure heartache and sorrow.

You must face humiliation and discouragement.

You work while others play.

You support those who have fallen.

You encourage the despairing.

You give directions to the lost.

You carry the burdens of many.

You weep for the suffering.

You laugh with the happy.

You calm the angry.

You comfort the mourning.

You pray for wisdom.

You smile to the frowning.

You listen to the ideas of others.

You forgive those who hold grudges.

You are needed by many.

You are recognized by few.

You achieve the impossible.

You give credit to others.

You give all of yourself to be a leader.

But you ask yourself every day,

"Is it worth it?"

But it is, when you make a difference in the life of another.

For that tilts the scales of sacrifice.

And it makes being a leader

One of the greatest privileges in the world. ★

True Leaders Never Lose
By David Tukey

After spending two years working to address students concerns about campus life through the Undergraduate Student Government at Princeton, I decided to run for President of the Student Body, thinking that such a title would better allow me to build the relationships and implement the programs I came to deem necessary.

I ran against four other students and won a spot in the run-off election. A year after losing that run-off election, I am thankful that I did not have the pressure of that title to shoulder as I worked toward establishing and expanding my priority programs. Not only would I not have had the time to accomplish the things I have done, but I would not have had the ability to cultivate the relationships that are such a defining aspect of the Princeton experience. Below is what you might call my 'concession' email:

Hi Everyone,

A few hours ago, I got a voicemail from Spence telling me that I had not won the election. An ensuing phone call confirmed that news and let me know that the margin of Joe's victory was indeed substantial.

Certainly, I'm disappointed, embarrassed, and perhaps even a little confused, but I want you to note that at no point in the paragraph above did I use any derivative of the word "lose".

Because, to me, talk of losing is talk of futility, talk of waste, talk of despair, and I certainly would not use any of those words to describe this experience.

Call me cliché, but this experience affords me strength of character along with the chance to get to know people at Princeton that I would have never met otherwise. In addition, it has taught me, once again, that hard work is truly the means by which things come to fruition. Above all, though, it's made me realize that I'm one of the luckiest dudes on Earth — I've got you.

Each one of you helped me in one way or another. Believe me, I know how valuable time is around here, and for you to have spared even five minutes to help me out is something that I absolutely will not forget.

The few people I've talked to thus far have asked me the questions I know I would ask anyone in my position: "How are you?" "What are you going to do now?" Well, to save the rest of you the awkwardness, I'm fine. I told everyone this was a win-win situation.

My victory tonight is a gift of time. There are substantive opportunities over the next year that I would not have been able to take full advantage of if I had won this election. And, now, I can better pursue what I decided before to be the essence of my Princeton experience — the friendships we cultivate.

Forgive me, please let me be didactic in closing, with what I'm taking from this. Be gracious in victory and magnanimous in the face of disappointment, taking as much personal responsibility as possible. Because there's always somebody watching, waiting to show you that everything happens for a reason.

Nuthin but love,

David ★

Just Belong
Author Unknown

Are you an active member?
The kind that would be missed,
Or are you just contented
That your name is on the list?
Do you attend the meetings
And mingle with the flock?
Or do you stay at home
And criticize and knock?
Do you ever go and visit
A member who is sick
Or leave the work to just a few
And talk about the clique?
Come to meetings often,
And help with hand and heart.
Don't be just a member
But take an active part,
Think it over, member,
You know right from wrong.
Are you an active member,
Or do you just belong? ★

The Day I Was A Dipstick
By Anthony J. D'Angelo

During my junior year of college I was on my way to attend a regional leadership conference in Cape May, New Jersey. I was looking forward to the conference as a great learning experience, as I was the newly elected Treasurer of the Student Government Association at West Chester University of Pennsylvania. I had planned to carpool with the other SGA executive members, but it was a hectic day for me on campus and I was running late. So I decided to drive solo to the conference.

About 50 miles away from the conference site, I peered down at my gas gauge and saw the low fuel warning light illuminated. I was running on empty. Fortunately I spotted a gas station ahead and pulled in to refuel. As I turned into the station, I attempted to pull up to an island that was self-service. Then I remembered that in the state of New Jersey motorists are not allowed to pump their own gas. You must wait for a station attended to pump your gas for you. So I turned the ignition off and waited. And waited. And waited.

"What the heck is going on? Let's Go! I'm late as it is." I vented in frustration. But nobody heard me, for I had all the windows up because the temperatures were in the low teens. All one could hear was a blustery icy-cold wind whip through the air.

Just as I was about turn the car on to get some heat, a knock at my window startled me. Finally! It was the attendant. As I rolled down the window I could feel the ice-cold air sting my face.

"What'll it be?" questioned the man.

"Fill it up with 87. Oh and can you check the oil? Thank you."
Every time I got gas, I made it a habit to check my oil. For the
car I was driving was my mom's former family truckster, a 1979
Pontiac Station Wagon. It was not going to hold up much
longer and it drank oil like a camel drinks water. As I popped
the hood, out of my review mirror, I could see the man putting
the nozzle in my tank.

"Boy that guy is crazy. He's gotta be freezing out there," I
thought to myself.

The gas station attendant was dressed in his outdoor gear. He
wore a long forest green coat and black wool hat yet he wore
no gloves. Instead he had his hands tucked up inside of his coat
sleeves so as to keep them warm.

After inserting the nozzle and turning on the pump, he proceeded to walk in front of car and with one hand unlatched to
the hood and hoisted it up. During my wait I decided to review
my conference itinerary to see what in store for me. After about
five minutes or so, the sound of the automatic pump shut-off
jolted me from my reading induced trance. I glanced up to see
my hood still up.

I started to get impatient again, "What the heck is this guy
doing?" I could only see his waist through the small narrow
strip of view that I had between the hood and my dash; his
hand still holding the hood, white knuckle bones and all.

My inner voices began to clamor, "I'm gonna be really late. The nerve of this guy! What in the world is taking him so long. I've gotta say something, I've gotta do something. How dare he make me wait around like this. I tell him!"

So I quickly swung the car door open, hopped out of my seat, slammed the door behind me and rushed to the front of the car. I shouted, "What in the heck is taking you so long!"

Before the man could respond, I looked up and saw his one hand holding up the hood and looked down to see his "free hand". To much of my embarrassment, I saw that it wasn't a hand, it was a metal hook, a prostheses. It had become entwined in the car's engine. The man was simply standing there waiting patiently for one of his co-workers to assist him. He said that he did not want to trouble me.

It was not the man with the hook who was handicapped that day. It was me and my handicap was my impatience and my ignorance. Looking back today, I don't even remember the leadership conference, but I have never forgotten the lesson I learned that day. ★

"Focus On Progress,
Not On Perfection."

Dan Sullivan,
Creator of the Strategic Coach®

A Quandary of Jewels
By Daniel E. Ashlock Jr.

Have you been caught by this quandary of leadership — if the outcome is not perfect then the effort was wasted?

There once was a princess who was enamored with jewelry. She loved opals, pearls, emeralds, diamonds, onyx, rubies, silver, and gold. But what this princess desired more than anything in the world was a blue sapphire. She sent word to her royal subjects that a contest was underway.

"The one who brings me the biggest, brightest sapphire will become my husband," she exclaimed, "and will thus one day help me rule this great land!"

Thus the race began. Men searched the rivers. Boys who were barely in their teens scoured the valleys and hills. Still others sifted the sand on the beach and in the fields. A whole year passed and princess grew cranky. She sent new words to her royal subjects. "I am discontent without a sapphire. I have rubies as red as blood, emeralds as green as the grass and silver as shiny as the full moon. Yet, I desire nothing more than one sapphire as blue as the sky. Bring me a sapphire and I will make you my husband!"

The royal subjects began to search anew. Every mother nagged her son to spend each waking moment on the hunt for the most dazzling sapphire. The only thing on every mind was the hunt for a sapphire.

One lad of sixteen had been searching in caves and gullies for a sapphire. After an unusually long hike, he slept soundly and encountered an inspiring dream.

He discarded his quest for the sapphire and began the most secretive project in his father's workshop. Upon the completion of his work, the lad set off to hold court with the princess. When he found her, the princess was eager to see his sapphire. "Is your sapphire as pure as the sky?" she asked.

"I'm afraid that I cannot answer your question. Only you will be able to tell if what I have to offer is acceptable to your yearnings," countered the lad. "Close your eyes and trust me."

The princess was amused by his playfulness and discretely closed her eyes. The lad opened his pack and took out a pair of glasses fashioned with cerulean lenses. He gently placed the spectacles on the princess then pulled a clear pebble from his pocket and placed it in her hands.

"Princess, before you open your eyes, take a deep breath."

After exhaling, the princess opened her eyes and saw the most beautiful gem she had ever seen. Then she realized that everything in her vision appeared as blue as the sky. "What a clever lad you are. You not only brought me a spectacular sapphire, you also turned my whole world the most brilliant blue. I shall never spend one waking hour without you by my side." Keeping her promise to the royal kingdom, the lad and the princess were married and grew old together.

Do you search endlessly for the sapphire or do you find inspiration in your dreams? Perfection is in the eye of the beholder. Avoid getting stuck in the dilemma of trying to fulfill what others deem perfect. When you are satisfied with your efforts, hold them up for all to appreciate. What you have to offer as a leader is certainly a jewel! ★

Getting An Education, Not Just A Degree
By Anthony J. D'Angelo

Before setting off to college my father sat me down and shared this memorable story with me. It is one that I shall never forget. Now my father is not college educated himself, yet he possessed more wisdom and insight than most college professors I ever met. After you read this story you'll know what I mean.

"There is an old story of a boilermaker who was hired to fix a huge steamship boiler system that was not working well. After listening to the engineer's description of the problems and asking a few questions he went to the boiler room. He looked at the maze of twisting pipes, listened to the thump of the boiler and the hiss of escaping steam for a few minutes, and felt some pipes with his hands. Then he hummed softly to himself, reached into his overalls and took out a small hammer, and tapped a bright red valve, once. Immediately the entire system began working perfectly, and the boilermaker went home. When the steamship owner received a bill for $1,000 he complained that the boilermaker had only been in the engine room for fifteen minutes and requested an itemized bill. So the boilermaker sent him a bill that read the following:

For tapping the hammer:	.50
For knowing where to tap:	$ 999.50
TOTAL:	$1,000.00

"Tony," he said, "I want you to go to college so that you can get your degree, but more importantly I want you to return with an education. Make certain that you find opportunities that tap you and your potential. Promise not to settle for anything less than that."

Years later as I reflect on this story, I can honestly say that I got my degree from lessons I learned in the classroom. But I got my education from my lessons learned as a student leader. I would not trade the latter for anything. ★

These Are The Days
Author Unknown, Submitted by Debra Lamp

Sometime in between moving
into the dorm and begging for an ID.
Somewhere in the middle of an 8 o'clock class,
and watching Friends on our 8 inch TV.

Sometime after the night you forgot,
with the girl you don't remember.
Maybe before the five tests in three days,
or the party every night in September.

Sometime in the car on the way to
California for the road trip of the year.
After class gets out with that bad TA,
after you finish the last warm beer.

Shortly after you figured
out this new college thing.
And after you stopped dreaming about,
the fun a 21 ID would bring.

Maybe the morning after you
pulled the all nighter, but finally got the paper done,
Or maybe when you can't remember,
the last Sunday night you had fun.

Somewhere between the day you met your first roommate, and
you thought you got one of the duds,
And the day 4 years later when he's still your roommate,
and he's one of your best buds.

Definitely after you realized how lucky you are,
to have such a great group of friends,
And after you get that sick feeling in your stomach,
wondering what will happen when it ends.

Maybe on the beach for spring break,
hot sun, tan bodies, cold beer,
Maybe after you started looking for a job,
and your happy world turned to fear.

Soon after you discovered there's just
not enough time, to do everything you should.
But not before you realized
Thanksgiving dinner, never tasted so good.

Sometime after the day your parents
came to visit, so you were forced to make your bed.
Or the morning after a tough night at the bars,
and you can't believe the things you've said.

Sometime after you enjoy the
beautiful weather, though it means missing a class.
Probably after laughing on Homecoming weekend,
watching old alumni drunk off their collective ass.

Sometime between day one and year four,
the best years of your life were spent.
And looking back with a smile and a sigh,
you wonder where those years went.

You try to figure out who made you
a victim of the most serious crime.
You offer a reward for any information
Leading to the one who stole time.

The day is coming closer and closer,
until one day it will be your last.
And someone is guilty of doing this to you,
the years have gone way too fast.

Sometime when you were too busy to notice,
happy as a new born pup. Someone came along
and did the unthinkable, somebody grew us up.

So with the above in mind, I promise myself with this oath,
Even though emotions of joy and sorrow move through me both,

I will keep an open mind. I will keep things in perspective.
I will smell the roses. I will not wait until tomorrow.
I will not graduate only to become what I despise.
I will not allow college to have been the best years of my life,
for each year shall be better than the last. I will not go quietly.
I will remember that "this too shall pass"
I will squeeze the most out of this life.
I will do what you think can't be done.
I will live today. These Are The Days. ★

Discover Your Own Acres of Diamonds
By Russell Conwell

Not far from the River Indus, there once lived a Persian farmer by the name of Ali Hafed, who owned a large farm with orchards and gardens. He was a wealthy, contented man— contented because he was wealthy and wealthy because he was contented. One day he was visited by a traveling merchant from the East. The man sat by the fires and told Ali Hafed how vast rich veins of diamonds were being discovered all over the continent. Ali Hafed dreamed how he could be even wealthier if he only had diamonds.

That night Ali Hafed went to bed a poor man—poor because he was discontented and discontented because he thought he was poor. "I want a diamond mine", he repeated to himself throughout the night.

The next day Ali Hafed decided to stake his claim. He sold his farm and left his family in a neighbor's care as he went off to search for diamonds. He searched all across the land. He went to the Middle East and found none. He went to Europe and found none. When the last of his money had been spent, he stood in rags at Spain's Bay of Barcelona, watching the waves roll in. Soon the penniless, hopelessly wretched man cast himself into the oncoming tide and sank beneath the water, never to rise again.

One day the man who purchased Ali Hafed's farm led his camel into the garden to drink. As the camel lapped the brook's clear water, the man noticed a curious flash in the shallow stream's white sands. Reaching into the water, he withdrew a black pebble with an eye of light that reflected all the colors of the rainbow. He took the curious stone into the house, put it on the mantel and returned to his chores.

Some days later, he was visited by the traveling merchant. The moment the merchant saw the gleam from the mantel, he rushed to it. "There's a diamond here!" he shouted. "A diamond! Has Ali returned?"

"No, he hasn't returned, and that's no diamond," the new owner answered. "It's nothing but a stone from out there in the garden."

"I know a diamond when I see one," the merchant insisted. "I tell you that's what it is. It is a beautiful diamond."

Together they rushed to the garden stream. They stirred the white sands with their fingers and, lo, discovered more stones, even more beautiful and valuable than the first. Thus the diamond mine of Golcanda was discovered, the most magnificent in history.

For decades, every shovelful from near that stream revealed gems that would decorate the crowns of monarchs. Had Ali Hafed remained at home and dug in his own garden instead of wandering aimlessly into a life of frustration, poverty, and suicide in a strange land, he would have had acres of diamonds.

Take a look around. You're already standing on your own acres
of diamonds- your campus.

Editor's Note: Russell Conwell, one of the original American moti-
vational speakers became world renowned for his famous message
Acres of Diamonds. He led a small group of volunteers who turned
a night school in their church basement into Temple University in
Philadelphia, PA. This momentous accomplishment took years of
sacrifice and effort. To raise money for books, facilities and faculty,
Conwell became a prominent lecturer and an author of 16 books.
He gave his famous lecture some six thousand times over two
decades. It was the spellbinding "Acres of Diamonds," whose mes-
sage is as relevant today as it was when he traveled the nation
sharing it so that he could build Temple University. This single
story led to the creation of a university & many more like it. ★

"Our deepest fear is not that we are inadequate. Our deepest fear is that we are powerful beyond measure. It is our Light, not our darkness, that most frightens us."

Marianne Williamson

Women Who Dare & Who Helped Us All
By Anthony J. D'Angelo

It has been almost a decade since I was a student who served on the presidential search committee for my college. I was a student leader at West Chester University in Pennsylvania, who was selected to represent the students of my campus in this very important endeavor.

I was a provincially minded 19 year old white heterosexual male from middle class America, and I really never knew how fortunate I was. Not until nine years later, when I visited Seneca Falls, New York did I truly comprehend this privileged reality of other "white guys" like me.

In Seneca Falls, I discovered a place that every man, woman and child should experience, The Women's Rights National Historical Park, The Birth Place of The Women's Rights Movement.

Here are some little-known facts which helped me to understand the educational plight of American women, from both yesterday and today.

In 1788, the town of Northampton, Massachusetts voted "to be at no expense for the schooling of girls."

In 1790, Boston girls were allowed to attend public schools only in summer months, and only if there were seats left vacant by boys.

New England led the nation in establishing female seminaries in the 1820's and 1830's. By 1840, nearly every woman could read and write in this region. In the South, 20 percent of white woman could neither read nor write.

In 1837 the only 2 schools which women could pursue a college degree were Georgia Female College and Oberlin College. And even though Oberlin opened its doors to women in 1837, it would not allow female students to speak in public until 1856, and its library remained strictly segregated by sex until the 1890's.

In 1837 Mary Lyon founded Mount Holyoke. Lucretia Mott helped found Swarthmore College in 1864. Sophia Smith financed the establishment of Smith College in 1875.

In 1897, South Carolina University student Laura Bateman was elected president of the freshman class, but was asked to resign because her sex made her unfit for the job.

Only 7% of high-school-aged children attended school in 1900, but woman made up 60% of the graduates.

In 1910, 19% of all college faculty and administrators were women. This peaked in 1930, when 32% were women, and returned to 19% by 1960.

Women earned 18% of all doctoral degrees in 1930, 10% of doctoral degrees in 1950. By 1990, women earned one-third of doctoral degrees granted in the United States.

In 1856, Lucy Stone wrote, "Our demand that Harvard and Yale Colleges should admit women, thought not yielded, only wants for a little more time." It took over a century for the Ivy League schools to accept women students. Harvard started allowing Radcliffe undergraduates to attend classes with men in the 1940s. Yale and Princeton admitted their first women students in the late 1960s and early 1970s, and Columbia followed in 1983.

Before the 1970s, there were no athletic scholarships for women; by 1990, over 10,000 were offered.

From 1975 to 1990, the number of woman college presidents doubled, with woman heading more 300 of the nation's 3,000 colleges and universities.

As you can see, we've come a long way.
But there is a lot more for us to do.
Do your part; Each of us, for all of us.

Editor's Note: In the Fall of 1992, Dr. Madeleine Wing Adler was named the first female president of West Chester University of PA. Dr. Adler celebrates her 10th year of service in 2002.

For information about
The Women's Rights National Historical Park,
Call: 315-568-9039 or visit www.nps.gov/wori
Please visit this place at least once in your lifetime. ★

The Sense of A Goose
Author Unknown

When you see geese flying along in "V" formation, you might consider what science has discovered as to why they fly that way. As each bird flaps its wings, it creates uplift for the bird immediately following. By flying in "V" formation, the whole flock adds at least 71 percent greater flying range than if each bird flew on its own.

Student leaders who share a common vision and a sense of community can get anywhere they're going more quickly and easily because they are traveling on the thrust of one another.

When a goose falls out of formation, it suddenly feels the drag and resistance of trying to go at it alone--- and quickly gets back into formation to take advantage of the lifting power of the bird in front.

If we as student leaders have as much sense as a goose, we will stay in formation with those people who are headed in the same way we are.

When the head goose gets tired, it rotates back in the wing and another goose flies point.

As student leaders we need to learn how to delegate and let go when doing demanding jobs. Even if we are not geese flying south.

Geese honk from behind to encourage those up front to keep up their speed.

What message do we give others when we honk from behind?

Lastly when a goose gets sick or is wounded by gunshot, and falls out of formation, two other geese fall out with that goose and follow it down to lend help and protection. They stay with the fallen goose until it is able to fly or until it dies; and only then do they launch out on their own, or with another formation to catch up with their group.

If we have the sense of a goose,
we will stand by each other like that. ★

Are You Strong Enough To Handle The Critics?
By *Theodore Roosevelt*

It is not the critic who counts, not the man who points out how the strong man stumbles or where the does of deeds could have done them better. The credit belongs to the man who is actually in the arena, whose face is marred by dust and sweat and blood, who strives valiantly, who errs and comes short again and again because there is no effort without error and shortcomings, who knows the great devotion in the end the high achievement of triumph and who at worst, if he fails while daring greatly, knows his place shall never be with those timid and cold souls who know neither victory nor defeat. ★

Complications
By Mark Walker

I really don't know what went wrong; I turned the corner and pressed on the gas pedal. Before I knew it we were upside down and the warm flow of blood began to sting my eyes. I think the cop said something like, "Due to the rain and the fact that you had seven people in your car you just lost control." The words flowed out of his mouth like he was a character on an infomercial. I wasn't buying it. How could I have lost control. I starred at the underside of my car as the rain sizzled off the red-hot parts of my engine. I remember thinking how small and odd my car looked in its unnatural position.

When I was seven, my G.I. JOE action figures were all that mattered to me. I must have had fifty of the damn things. I would march my armies across the living room carpet and infiltrate the secret hiding place of the enemy. My soldiers would climb up the couch and fight to victory from cushion to cushion. We fought battles in the front yard jungle, the arctic swimming pool climate, and the ever-dreaded battle in the microwave. We suffered many casualties in that one and I went to bed with a sore bottom.

When I was younger, a bad day consisted of sending a note over to Liz Ketchum with the words, DO YOU LIKE ME? CHECK YES, NO, MAYBE and having it sent back with a check in the NO box. Now a bad day is, waking up at 3:30 a.m. to go bail my buddy out of jail for getting a DUI in the parking lot of Taco Bell.

He had been drinking and decided to "make a run for the border." Now he will probably never be able to fulfill his dream of being in the FBI.

So what happened? When did things get so complicated? How did we go from riding bikes to the end of the earth, pulling little girls pig tails for fun, eating candy until we threw up, watching Saturday morning cartoons in our Superman pajamas with the cape and built in booties to watching our friends lose their parents or other friends? When did things change?

"Did you hear? A guy got shot in Main Hall. A girl got killed in a car accident on the way back to school. Two people got robbed in the student union. They actually crashed planes into the Twin Towers. Did you hear? Did you hear? Did you hear?"

One time I was starring at my dog Skip. He was lying on the front deck. The sun was making the blackness of his coat shine brilliantly. I thought to myself, as he reared his head up to lick his paw, "What a life. Skip's only worry is that he has to wait for someone to open a door for him because he doesn't have an opposable thumb." No worries. But if a closed door to him is like me locking my keys in my car then it all must be relative.

So is there no way out of the worries and complications in life?

You're born. Learn to walk. Learn to talk. Learn to pee. Learn to read. Learn to write. Go to high school. Get zits. Get laid (hopefully). Get detention. Learn to drive. Learn to crash. Learn to love. Learn to cry. Get into college. Get smart. Get a degree. Get a life.

I don't know about you, but my life and every point of it seems like a life changing monumental event. From the time I crashed my first car to wondering if I'll graduate at all. But I think I've figured out that at those points in life, at those very moments that seem so important, to think of life five years from then. Will you even remember what happened? Will it have really mattered as much as you thought?

I guess what I mean is that when we grow up our responsibilities grow up. That makes life seem more complicated. But they way I see it, is that its no more complicated than a three year old trying to climb the kitchen counter to get to the cookie jar. We are just older and our cookie jars are just a little higher. ★

The Purpose of Student Leaders
By Elizabeth Randazzese

Why do college campuses have student leaders? Is it to make an impact on the decisions, policies and activities of the campus community? Absolutely. But there is an even more important reason for student leaders. These are the students who choose to lead when no one else knows how to.

I don't think the function of a student leader is to have all the answers, solutions or ideas. Instead, a student leader should have the ability to inspire others despite the circumstances. Think about it: As a student leader, when things in your organization are going well, it is so easy to be positive and enthusiastic, right? Your group just had a great turnout for elections, you just organized a phenomenal fundraiser, or your group was honored in the campus newspaper. Those times are great. Everyone is perfectly happy, right? Trying to inspire others in times of prosperity is relatively easy.

But what happens, when your organization is not "riding so high." When your group is faced with difficult situations, or even worse charged with horrible allegations that are not true? Those are the times that optimism is hard to find among your members. It is in that unique moment of despair that the student leader is needed. It is in that moment that the group needs a word of encouragement. It is in that moment that an organization can pull together or pull apart.

It is in this moment that the student leader becomes a true catalyst for transforming a challenging situation into an opportunity to learn and grow. This is the ultimate way we can serve our campus as student leaders. It is not about having the right speech, the right answer, or the right idea. It is about leading when no one knows what will come next. It is about leading despite challenging circumstances. It is about choosing to lead when no one knows how to, and in the process, teaching others the meaning of leadership. ★

The Chopsticks of Heaven & Hell
By Anthony J. D'Angelo

There is a poignant Zen story about a person who visited both heaven and hell. In both places, the visitor saw many people seated at a table on which many delicious foods were laid out. Chopsticks over a meter long were tied to their right hands, while their left hands were tied to their chairs.

In hell, however much they stretched out their arms, the chopsticks were too long for them to get food into their mouths. They grew impatient and got their hands and chopsticks tangled with one another. The delicacies were scattered here and there.

In heaven, on the other hand, people happily used the long chopsticks to pick out someone else's favorite food and feed it to him, and in turn they were being fed by others as they all enjoyed their meal in harmony.

As student leaders we have the power to create our campus culture. It can be heaven or it can be hell. The decision is ours. ★

Lessons from a Fly
By Dan Oltersdorf

I was one of few people I knew in college who "had it all together" as a freshman, and knew exactly what I wanted to do with my life. I knew beyond a shadow of a doubt that I was going to become a Doctor of Chiropractic. Of course this was after I previously "knew" that I wanted to go to trade school, among many other aspirations I had as I grew up. However, this goal was different because I was doing something about it.

By my third year at Colorado State University, I had finished most of my prerequisite coursework for Chiropractic College including suffering through Organic Chemistry II. There was only one problem. I wasn't as "together" as I would have liked to believe. I was beginning to question my aspirations of Chiropractic medicine. I was now a junior at CSU, taking courses in Exercise and Sport Science, and had almost finished my pre-med requirements for Chiropractic school. I had visited six Chiropractic colleges from all over the country the previous summer, and was on my way to following my dream.
Or was I? This is where my experience as a student leader began to change my life.

During my freshman year, I became very involved on campus, and by my junior year, I had a job on campus, was president of a student organization, and was involved in several others. While I hadn't previously given it much thought, I began to note that I was truly enjoying these experiences, and they were shaping me as a leader and as a person. I began to realize that I was making a difference in people's lives, and that I loved to work with college students. I started to wonder if a career in Chiropractic medicine was really the direction I wanted to go. I struggled internally with this nagging question for weeks. Now that I was in my third year of college, I told myself it was too late to change directions. I was thoroughly committed to my current course, and even if I changed direction, what would I do?

As I struggled with this feeling of uncertainty, I continued on with my leadership experiences on campus. During this time, I was torn between the well-planned path I was on, and the unclear but compelling alternatives that seemed to be calling me in other directions. It was soon that a few unlikely messengers would begin to define my direction, including one which flew right into my life.

During the following summer I became an orientation leader. As part of the orientation training process, I had the opportunity to go to a conference called NODA. At the conference, I had the wonderful opportunity to hear a speaker by the name of Joe Martin. Professor Martin spoke about purpose. As he talked about finding, accepting, and living one's God-given purpose, my mind began to race. After Joe's presentation, I went and spoke with him and he asked me a series of questions that would begin to change my life. We spoke for nearly an hour after his presentation, and I wildly scribbled notes on a small piece of paper, as Joe asked me defining questions which would cause me to further question my current direction and begin to define a new one. He helped me to realize that I need-ed to actively seek and define my purpose, my passions, and my direction.

Back at Colorado State, I continued to wonder what all of this questioning and uncertainty meant. One of my favorite spots (later to become the site of my proposal to the woman who is now my wife) was a small non-denominational chapel on Colorado State's campus. Danforth chapel was a small building with a heated stone floor that I would sometimes sit on and reflect. Danforth was my momentary "retreat" from the hectic pace of campus life.

One cold day as I sat in Danforth, I was reflecting, and asking myself "what is it that I am supposed to do," an unlikely messenger came to my side. I was sitting on the heated stone floor with my back against the wall, and my backpack to my left side, when I heard a buzzing noise. For a moment, I thought there was some type of electrical problem, and wondered about the source of this intermittent buzzing sound. I started scanning the small room when the noise sounded again. This time, I realized it was right beside me. I looked down on the floor and saw a fly stuck on its back on the floor. The buzzing was coming from its futile attempts to right itself. Rather than swatting the fly, which would usually have been my first instinct, I reached down and nudged it with my finger. As I did this, it immediately flew away and I returned to my musings.

No sooner had I looked away from the fly than a flood of thoughts rushed into my mind. I realized that what I had just done to the fly was what I wanted to do with my life; that is, I wanted to help people to fly. I could think of so many who simply needed a little nudge to help them to achieve their potential. At the same time, I thought of the many mentors and leaders in my life who had given me that same nudge and were helping me to "fly" as well. I thought of people like my advisors, Jack MacDonald and Kyle Parker; my teachers, Barb Kistler and Martha Fosdick; and of my new friend and mentor Joe Martin who had "nudged me" to start living with "purpose, passion, and power." Since then, countless others continue to give me the "nudges" I need to fly to the next level in my potential as I continue to pursue my purpose.

This "fly inspired epiphany" gave me a pictorial description of what I wanted to do with my life. While it took a few appointments with a career counselor and the advice of many of my mentors, I soon began to redefine my direction. I changed my major to Human Development and became an Orientation Leader, then a Resident Assistant. It wasn't long before I realized I could make a career of working with students, and I am now pursuing a career in Higher Education, where my goal continues to be represented by the picture of that little fly. Many people in my life have given me the "nudges" I have needed to get off of my back, and my aim is to provide that same assistance to others through my career in Higher Education.

Being a student leader is a challenge and an opportunity. It is a way to learn, to grow, and to serve. There is no other experience in college life that more effectively shapes one's college experience and one's future opportunities. Most importantly, there is no better way to "learn to fly" and afford others with the opportunity and the incentive to do the same.

Editor's Note: Since his "fly inspired epiphany", Dan Oltersdorf has gone on to nudge thousands of other student leaders. In 1998 he created www.ResidentAssistant.com and began working on a little book called, Inspiration for RAs. This book began help to launch The Inspiration Book Series™. It looks like the fly has helped us all to fly a little higher. ★

"There Is No Chance, No Destiny, No Fate That Can Circumvent, Hinder Or Control The Firm Resolve Of A Committed Soul."

Ella Wheeler Wilcox

Just Because It's Tradition, Doesn't Make It Right.
By Anthony J. D'Angelo

One day a young girl watched her mother prepare a ham for baking. At one point the daughter asked, "Mom, why did you cut off both ends of the ham?"

"Well, because my mother always did," said the mother.
"But, why?"
"I don't know—let's go ask Grandma."

So they went to Grandma's and asked her, "Grandma, when you prepare the ham for baking, you always cut off both ends—why did you do that?"

"My mother always did it," said Grandma.
"But, why?"
"I don't know—let's go ask Great-grandma." So off they went to Great-grandma's.

"Great-grandma, when you prepare the ham for baking, you always cut off both ends—why did you do that?"

"Well, "Great-grandma said, "the pan was too small."

Whether you are running for president, recruiting new members or simply conducting your weekly meeting, ask yourself, "Why do we do it this way?" And remember, just because it is tradition, doesn't make it right. ★

Leadership Demonstrated By Picking Up Trash
By George Brelsford

Many years ago when I was a new professional, I had landed a job at a small school in the northeast. At this school part of my job was to supervise the resident assistant staff. One of my RAs was a young woman named Keri Krisman. Keri was a small person barely five feet tall and might have weighed 100 pounds if her pockets were full of rocks.

Keri worked hard, never slacked off and took her leadership position very seriously. What made Keri special was that she picked up trash. I noticed Keri picking up trash one night as I was walking the campus. As time went by I noticed that Keri always picked up trash whenever she was walking on campus. She did not make a big production of it she simply picked up whatever trash she happened to see as she was going to class, or heading off to dinner or making her duty rounds.

So I found myself emulating her behavior. On my way to work or on my way home, whenever I walked the campus I picked up trash. I also noticed that the students on Keri's floor not only took pride in the appearance of their living area they were also picking up trash. Whenever you walked with Keri she picked up trash so you picked up trash as well.

Soon it was more the norm to see people on campus take the time to throw trash into a trashcan rather than simply tossing it on the ground. We all took pride in our little campus.

Keri worked on my staff for three years. In addition to picking up trash Keri was a master of disciplinary confrontations. Little Keri could talk to any of our 250-pound football players about their behavior. Her personal integrity was so great that she was always taken seriously and respected.

Leadership is not always about crises most often it is about doing the right thing for the right reason every day. Keri picked up trash and in the process developed her personal integrity, modeled a positive behavior, and encouraged others to grow and develop as people. This is true leadership.

I have not seen or talked to Keri in about 20 years. Wherever she is and whatever she is doing, I bet she is picking up trash. ★

A Memo To Student Leaders
By The Boss

To: You, A Student Leader

From: The Boss

Subject: On Being A Student Leader

Reference: Life

I am God. Today I will be handling all of your problems. Please remember that I do not need you help.

If life happens to deliver a situation to you that you cannot handle, do not attempt to resolve it. Kindly put it in the SFGTD (Something For God To Do) Box. All situations will be resolved, but in MY time, not yours.

Once the matter is placed into the box, do not hold onto it by worrying about it. Instead, focus on all the wonderful things that are present in your life now.

If you find yourself frustrated with the administration's new policy of the month; Don't despair. There are students on your campus who don't even care about such matters.

Should you bomb an exam, because you were working on a new event until 2 a.m. the night before. Don't despair. Think of all those students who have not experienced all that you have.

Should you despair over a relationship gone bad; Think of the person who has never known what it's like to love and be loved in return.

Should you grieve the passing of yet another weekend; think of the woman in dire straits, working twelve hours a day, seven days a week to feed her children.

Should your car break down, leaving you miles away from assistance: think of the paraplegic who would love the opportunity to take a walk.

Should you notice your first gray hair in the mirror: think of the cancer patient in chemo who wished she had hair to examine.

Should you find yourself at a loss and pondering what is life all about, asking what is my purpose? Be thankful. There are those who didn't live long enough to get the opportunity to ask such a question, let alone answer it.

Should you find yourself the victim of other people's bitterness, ignorance, smallness, insecurities; remember, things could be worse. You could be one of them!

Should you decide to share this with a friend; thank you, you may have touched their life in ways you will never know. ★

"You Have
A Serious Responsibility
Not To Be So Serious."

Maharishi Mahesh Yogi

How To Get An A On Your Final Exam
By Anthony J. D'Angelo

During my senior year in college, I had the opportunity to serve as a teacher's assistant. One of my roles was to administer and proctor the exams. The class was a freshman introductory course, which had well over 500 students.

The students were given four exams during the semester, and one cumulative final exam at the semester's end. Now in order to manage these 500 college freshman, I had to establish the rules. And the rules where: The exam would begin at exactly 9:00 a.m. The students would pick up their test booklet and a blue book and proceed to a seat of their choosing. They had exactly 50 minutes to complete the examination. At exactly 9:50 I would call out "Pencils down!" And everyone must stop writing immediately, put their pencils down, and proceed to the front of the room and turn in their bluebook. If you didn't put your pencil down at exactly 9:50 and turn in your blue-book you received an automatic F, no exceptions!

When final exam time came, the students where so indoctrinated with the system that I only needed to announce one warning at 9:40. So when the final minutes ticked I announced, "It is 9:40. You have 10 minutes until pencils down." Then at 9:50, I barked my last command for that semester, "It is 9:50. Pencils down! You know the rules!" And boom, all pencils went down. Just like always. And Shwish! all 500 students stood.... or was it only 499. Yes it was. Everyone filled the isle except for one sneaky guy, a guy way up in the nose bleed section.

He was just writing and writing away. I could see him up there, but he didn't think I could. Once again, I barked, "Pencils down everyone!" But he kept writing and writing, trying to beat my system. How dare he! Boy would I get him! At 9:58, as I began to organize the stacks of examination packets, I saw this young man running down the isle to surrender his to the table.

"Here Mr. D'Angelo, take my bluebook!" he huffed and puffed.

"I cannot except this. You know the rules. Pencils Down at 9:50 or you get an automatic F."

"Please Mr. D'Angelo, take my bluebook!"

"NO! You know I can't do that. It's against the rules."

"Please! Please! take my bluebook. I'm barely passing this class. My mom & dad will kill me if I have to repeat this class. Just take it no one will ever know!"

A tear began to stream down his cheek.
"I'm sorry, I just can't." I went back to the stacks, organizing them one by one. The young man just turned and walked away with his shoulders slumped.

Now with a stack of a 100 or so bluebooks in my arms, I watched the freshman walk up the stairs toward the exit. Just about at the halfway point, I saw him boldly turn around with great confidence, you might even say with a hint of arrogance.

He swiftly jogged down towards me. Surprised by this I turned and faced him, yet I was somewhat taken back and my arms seemingly froze with the stack of bluebooks in them.

He questioned softly "Mr. D'Angelo?, Do you know who I am?"

"Why no, and frankly I could care less." I said rather smugly.

"Are you sure you don't know who I am?"

He inquired with even greater confidence. I started to get a little concerned. Is this the Dean's son? What have I gotten myself into?

"No. I'm sorry I don't" (with a little hesitation in my voice.)

"Are you absolutely, 100% sure that you don't know who I am?!?!"

"For the last time-NO! I don't know who you are!"

Add so he said, "Well, THEN GOOD!" and he shoved his blue book into the middle of the stack and ran out the door! ★

*Editors' Note: This story by Anthony J. D'Angelo, originally appeared in Chicken Soup for The College Soul® and has gone on to inspire the creation of the classic scene in the hit movie Slackers. To view the scene visit:
www.apple.com/trailers/columbia/slackers.html*

Pebbles In Your Pockets
By Thomas W. Smith

A long, long time ago, three horsemen were crossing the desert one very dark night. As they came to a dry creek-bed, out of the darkness a loud voice commanded them to "Stop!"

Startled and instantly frightened, the riders did as they were told. The voice continued: "Dismount, pick up a handful of pebbles, put them in your pocket, and then ride on. At sunrise you will both very happy and very sad."

Again, the riders did as commanded. Then they mounted up, spurred their horses forward, and they didn't stop until the sun rose. When they reached into their pockets, they found that a miracle had occurred...the pebbles had turned to diamonds, rubies, sapphires, emeralds and other precious gems. Then they remembered the words of the mysterious voice in the darkness the night before. They were both very happy and very sad— happy they had taken some pebbles, but very sad they had not taken more.

And so, student leaders, I urge you to fill your pockets with as many precious opportunities as you can to serve and grow and learn and make a difference. Not everyone gets these opportunities, but they are as valuable as jewels, and I assure you, that through your involvement in helping others, you'll grow rich in skills and experience. ★

When In Doubt Do What Gandhi Did
Author Unknown

As Gandhi stepped aboard a train one day, one of his shoes slipped off and landed on the track. He was unable to retrieve it as the train was moving. To the amazement of his companions, Gandhi calmly took off his other shoe and threw it back along the track to land close to the first. Asked by a fellow passenger why he did so, Gandhi smiled and said, "The poor man who finds the shoe lying on the track," he replied, "will now have a pair he can use." ★

"Be The Change You Want To See In The World."
Gandhi

The Secret to Leadership
By Elizabeth Randazzese

Throughout the years of my student leadership experiences, I had the opportunity to meet and interact with some of the most amazing student affairs professionals on campus. I was certainly blessed to foster relationships with some phenomenal people. In particular, there was one student affairs professional with whom I have maintained a special relationship since first meeting him.

It was during my freshman year when I got to know George, who was the Student Government Association Advisor. Every campus needs a "George." He was one of the most passionate, caring and supportive people on campus. Throughout the years, George shared with me his ideas on the importance of and meaning of leadership. But, it wasn't until my final week at Rowan that I was reminded of George's greatest leadership lesson of all.

During the final week of classes in the spring semester, George and I went out to lunch together. We chatted about Rowan, shared memories and discussed the new adventures I might face in graduate school. Then, I asked George a question that had been on my mind for a while. So I asked, "George you have seen my leadership abilities and skills from freshman to senior year in a variety of situations. What do you think is the one skill, the one ability, the one leadership quality that I need to improve?"

What was he going to say? I eagerly and patiently awaited his response. Surely, he was going to give me a list of skills that I can further develop for my future endeavors. He first smiled and then said, "The one area that you need to improve on is not really a skill, ability or a technique. Honestly, you need to see what others see. You need to see and realize that you are an excellent leader with lots of enthusiasm. You need to continue to have a strong sense of confidence in yourself as the effective leader you already are."

During my final days at Rowan University, George reminded me of an indispensable lesson about leadership, and more importantly about life. He taught me that the "secret to leadership" does not come from a title, a position, a skill, or a technique. The true secret to leadership is simply confidence and belief in self. He reminded that without belief in self, it doesn't matter how many "leadership skills" one has. ★

What Legacy Will You Leave?
By Anthony J. D'Angelo

In philosophy class I had professor who was the quintessential eccentric philosopher. His disheveled appearance was highlighted by a well worn tweed sport coat and poor fitting thick glasses, which often rested on the tip of his nose. Every now and then, as most philosophy professors do, he would go off on one of those esoterically and existential "what's the meaning of life" discussions. Many of those discussions would go no where, but there were a few that really hit home. This was one of them:

"Respond to the following questions by a show of hands," My professor instructed.

"How many of you can tell me something about your parents?" Everyone's hand went up.

"How many of you can tell me something about your grandparents?" About three fourths of the class raised their hands.

"How many of you can tell me something about your great-grandparents?" Two out of sixty students raised their hands.

"Look around the room," he said. "In just two short generations hardly any of us even know who our own great grandparents were. Oh sure, maybe we have a old tattered photograph tucked away in a musty cigar box or know the classic family story about how he walked 5 miles to school barefoot. But how many of us really know who they were, what they thought,

what they were proud of, what they were afraid of, or what they dreamed about? Think about that. Within three generations our ancestors are all but forgotten.
Will this happen to you?"

"Here's a better question. Look ahead three generations. You are long gone. Instead of you sitting in this room, now are your great grandchildren. What will they have to say about you? Will they know about you? Or will you be forgotten too? With the only memory of you being your teeth on their bookshelf."

"Is your life going to be a warning or an example? What legacy will you leave? The choice is yours. Class dismissed."

Nobody rose from their seat for a good fifteen minutes. ★

What Is A Leader?

By Stephen M. Vindigni

A leader is a student who works
all semester for a 60-minute show,
And even without a thank you
continues to prosper and grow.

A leader listens to a crying
friend in their moment of deepest sorrow,
And passes up a Friday evening
knowing there will always be tomorrow.

A leader is there when a program is
canceled due to the thoughtless rain,
And smiles even though his hard
work has gone down the drain.

A leader builds friendships with
anyone and everyone there is to meet,
And even those that may dislike
takes the time to stop and greet.

A leader picks up the pieces when
a fellow student chooses to relax,
And laughs carefree even when
he may be stressed to the max.

A leader helps the homeless and
less fortunate around the town,
And viewing the terrible circumstances
forces a grin rather than a frown.

A leader is a person who sees
the positive in you and me,
And aspires to benefit everyone
even though many do not agree.

A leader can be young, old,
beginner, expert, unwise or prudent,
A leader can be you and me—
learning to be a leader and a student. ★

Success
By Ralph Waldo Emerson

To laugh often and much;
to win the respect of intelligent people
and the affection of children;
to earn the appreciation of honest critics
and endure the betrayal of false friends;
to appreciate beauty, to find the best in others; to leave the
world a bit better, whether
by a healthy child, a garden patch
or a redeemed social condition;
to know even one life has breathed
easier because you have lived.
This is to have succeeded. ★

A Simple Lesson About Leadership
By Anthony J. D'Angelo

During my senior year of college, I took a class on organizational leadership. One day my professor decided to give us a pop quiz. The quiz consisted of ten simple fill in the blank questions regarding the subject matter we had been studying during the last few weeks. I breezed through the questions until I read the last one. "What is the first name of the woman who cleans this building?"

Surely this was some kind of joke. I had seen the cleaning woman several times, but how would I know her name?

I handed in my paper, leaving the last question blank. Before the class ended, one student asked if the last question would count toward our grade.

"Absolutely," the professor said. "If you truly desire to be a leader you must realize that you will meet many people. Each and every person is significant. They deserve your attention and care, even if all you do is smile and say hello."

I'll never forget that lesson. I also will never forget that her name was Hazel. ★

"We See The World
Not As It Is,
But Rather As We Are."

Johann Wolfgang
von Goethe

Seeking To Understand
By Brian Dassler

On an unseasonably warm early spring day in March 2001, I facilitated a discussion that left every person in the room changed. Those in the room remark now about how much they learned in the two-hour discussion, and having seen congruent action associated with these words I am certain the thirty students in the room did indeed change for the better.

As a student leader, I had the opportunity to serve as the lead instructor our campus's three-credit course for new orientation leaders. Our entire staff was required to take the course that emphasized personal growth and university information. For this reason, our syllabus was designed with diversity in mind. Like most colleges and universities, my school, the University of Florida, has struggled with its campus climate for minority students and more recently with the implications of race neutral admissions policies.

On this day we were talking about both. Orientation leaders had recently finished Ron Suskind's *A Hope in the Unseen: An American Odyssey from the Inner City to the Ivy League* and participated in a discussion facilitated by Associate Professor of Education Mary Howard-Hamilton. Building on the messages of Suskind's book about Washington, D.C. student Cedric Jennings, I began the discussion by asking the leaders about their high school experience.

As the still reserved staff slowly opened up with one another, a number of things happened simultaneously. A relatively large group of students who had experienced backgrounds of privilege began to have their views about equity and opportunity challenged by students who attended high schools where such 'givens' were denied. Synapses were firing rapidly as leaders began realizing:

- Advanced Placement courses are not uniformly available.
- All high schools are not maintained to adequate health and safety standards.
- Many students never see a computer in their high school.
- Not all guidance counselors encourage students to apply to college or take rigorous courses.
- Students of color could not have parents who are graduates of the institution because of the university's decades-old policy denying admission to African-Americans.
- It's not easy being the only person like you in a class of eight hundred, one hundred, or even thirty.

The orientation leaders became more dazed and confused than could be expected from individuals of their generation as the dialogue advanced.

We talked in detail about the 'senior year question.' In some places, "Where are you going to school next year" and others, "What are you doing next year?" The questions are indeed different, and our leaders started seeing patterns. Students of color, students from low socioeconomic backgrounds, and students attending urban high schools were consistently and emotionally testifying to the inequities and injustices they faced

daily, and students of privilege (and often ignorance) took note.
Our privileged leaders began to understand that the opportunity available to them was not and is not uniformly available in
our society, and is most often denied in communities of color.
The room was alive with energy as students listened to and
learned from one another. We had real dialogue, a true flow of
meaning. I said very little as students spoke for themselves. It
was by no means a happy dialogue because issues of social
injustice are anything but happy, but the dialogue was certainly
transcendent. The orientation leaders left the two-hour class
drained from the emotional peaks and valleys, and committed
with a sense of passion, commitment, and efficacy unparalleled
in my years as a student leader.

An orientation leader wrote to me several hours later about
returning to his residence hall to a conversation about affirma-
tive action he now felt obliged to enter. Another orientation
leader left in tears as she couldn't understand the overwhelming
nature of hate and injustice. A third orientation leader
approached me later and thanked me for helping him say what
had been in his heart for years.

In the required journal that week, all members of the staff
remarked how in two short hours they had grown as leaders
and as human beings. Once working that summer, the staff
received regular compliments from administrators, parents, and
students about their inclusive and progressive approach to their
roles as campus ambassadors.

As for me, I was able to watch and be a part of what I hope to be the first of many synergistic, transcendent moments in a long and healthy teaching career. It was a special spring day, and a brief time in our lives none of us will ever forget.

Editors Note: Brian Dassler was selected as the 2001 Student Leader of The Year, by Florida Leader Magazine. ★

If You Talk The Talk, You Better Walk The Walk.
By Anthony J. D'Angelo

There were two great orators of antiquity.

One was Cicero, the other Demosthenes.
One was a great speaker, the other was a great leader.

When Cicero was done speaking, people always
gave him a standing ovation and said,
"What a great speech!"

When Demosthenes was done,
people would march into battle.

This is the difference between
presentation & persuasion.

There are some people who
are good at talking the talk.
But there are only a few who
can get others to walk the walk.

Be One of The Few Who Do.
Walk The Talk & Get Others To Do The Same.
Be A Leader. ★

Leadership Is About Perspective, Not Position
By Frank Koch

Two battle ships assigned to the training squadron had been at sea on maneuvers in heavy weather for several days. I was serving on the lead battleship and was on watch on the bridge as night fell. The visibility was poor with patchy fog, so the captain remained on the bridge keeping an eye on all activities.

Shortly after dark, the lookout on the bridge reported, "Light bearing on the starboard bow."

"Is it steady or moving stern?" The captain called out.

The lookout replied, "Steady Captain!" Which meant both ships were on a dangerous collision course.

The captain then called to the signalman, "Signal that ship: We are on a collision course, advise you change course 20 degrees."

Back came a signal, "Advisable for you to change course 20 degrees."

The captain said, "Send, I'm a captain, change course 20 degrees."

"I'm a seaman second class." Came the reply, "You had better change course 20 degrees."

By that time the captain was furious. He spat out, "Send, I'm a battleship. Change course 20 degrees!"

Back came the flashing light, "I am a lighthouse."

The captain decided to change his course. ★

What Being A Student Leader Is All About
By Anthony J. D'Angelo

It's about doing what most people do at age 40
when you're only 20.

It's about getting a education and not just a degree.

It's about taking your Higher Education deeper.

It's about transcending political correctness
and striving for human righteousness.

It's about valuing your self-reliance
more than your social security.

It's about having a passion and
not about holding a position.

It's about building your reputation
not just your resume.

It's about being a windshield and not a bug.

It's about giving not getting.

It's about who you become, not what you get.

It's about leading yourself so that you can lead others.
It is about focusing 90% of your time on solutions
And only 10% of your time on problems.

It is about growing antennas, not horns.

It's about realizing that community service
is the rent we pay for the privilege
of living in this world.

It means getting along with yourself
so you can get along with others.

It is about labeling bottles and not people.

It is about scheduling your priorities
as well as prioritizing your schedule.

It's about making love an action verb.

It's about challenging the status quo
rather than accepting it.

It is about being a pragmatic idealist.

It's about nurturing your own strength
so you can be a source of strength.

It's about knowing that you are an X.
Which means you are not an unknown,
rather you are a multiplication factor.

You are not just a pebble in this pond.
You are a boulder in the ocean.

You are a student leader. ★

The Inspiration Book Series

The Sermons We See
By Edgar A. Guest

I'd rather see a sermon than hear one any day;
I'd rather you walk with me
than merely show me the way.

The eye is a better pupil
and more willing than the ear,
I find counsel is confusing
but examples always clear.

And best of the preachers
are men that live their creeds.
For to see the good in action
is what everyone needs.

I can soon learn how to do it
if you let me see it done.
I can watch your hands in action
but your tongue too fast may run.

And the lectures you deliver
maybe wise and ever true
but I'd rather get my lesson
by observing what you do.

For I might misunderstand you
and the good advice you give
but there is no misunderstanding
how you act and how you live. ★

Politics Is Doing The Popular Thing
Leadership Is Doing The Right Thing
By A Student Leader

The following is an actual letter which was received for *Inspiration for Greeks™*. The editors felt that this submission would serve all student leaders, not just Greeks. The author's name has been withheld upon request of the author.

Dear Tony,

My name is Chris and we talked at the Regional Greek Conference last week. You expressed an interest in my story and so I am writing it. The only concern is that the Fraternity will be looked at in a bad light and if written in the wrong manner might give a bad representation of all Fraternity and Sorority members.

Since you are a fellow Greek member I'm sure you understand how serious this could hurt the Greek Community if it is written poorly. I'm sure I can trust you, and that you would not want to hurt Greeks any more than I would. You and Bob, my advisor told me that this story was very important and that it would help show a positive role of Greek leaders.

I just ask that you please make sure that it is written in a confidential fashion because I could easily get expelled from my chapter if it is not. Even though this story may sound negative, I still love my Fraternity and I don't know what I would do if I were not a part of it. So here is my story:

One day my roommate came to me extremely upset. It seemed that his girlfriend's good friend had been sexually assaulted by one of my Fraternity brothers. The girlfriend did not know who the guy was because the girl would not tell his name. All that was know is that a rape kit had been done and a police report had been filed. They were not pursuing the report because the woman would not press charges. I tried to convince the woman to tell me who the guy was so I could have him expelled from my chapter. I did not want a guy like that in my Fraternity. Nor did I want this guy around any females I knew.

Two months later I received a phone call. It was the woman who had been assaulted. She wanted to speak with me. About ten minutes later I met the woman outside of my Fraternity house. We then proceeded to a park where the girl told me everything that had occurred the night in question, including the name of the guy who assaulted her.

I became very angry and called an emergency meeting of our elder members to decide what to do. As president I don't have the authority to expel members by myself, so the chapter was going to have to vote on the issue. It went to a chapter vote. Unfortunately his membership was not revoked.

As an older brother this was very frustrating for me. The majority of our members are very young and sometimes can believe too strongly in the concept of brotherhood. Because of this they sometimes can make the wrong decision. Also because of legalities all the facts could not be shared with them.

After the vote was read and the members decided to back the brother I became very frustrated. In my opinion I felt the brother did it. I could not deal with the fact that we were letting him stay. This went against every moral value I have. I could not go before my peers, or the entire Greek Community as a president making the statement that we were going to support this guy as a brotherhood. So I resigned from my office as President.

I don't think I did anything special and that is why when you asked me to write my story I was a little surprised. I just did what any decent person would have done. If people think what I did was special, then I hope this story inspires a few more people to stand up for what they believe in and never to sacrifice their values for anything or anyone.

Something quite ironic happened after I resigned. The brother who had allegedly assaulted the woman quit the fraternity and left town. I guess God takes care of those who sin after all. I hope this story helps someone out there, and shows them when people get put in a bad position; they can stand up and fight back. ★

The Golden Rules For Living & Leadership
Author Unknown

If you open it, close it.

If you turn it on, turn it off.

If you unlock it, lock it up.

If you break it, admit it.

If you can't fix it, call in someone who can.

If you borrow it, return it.

If you value it, take care of it.

If you make a mess, clean it up.

If you move it, put it back.

If it belongs to someone else, get permission to use it.

If you don't know how to operate it, leave it alone.

If it's none of your business, don't ask questions.

If it will brighten someone's day, say it.

If it will hurt someone's reputation, keep it to yourself. ★

There Are Professors and Then There Are Educators
By Anthony J. D'Angelo

When I asked my Biology Professor,
"What Do You Teach?" He said, "Biology."
When I asked my Director of Student Activities,
"What Do You Teach?" She said, "Students."

When I asked my Statistics Professor
"What Do You Teach?" She said, "Statistics."
When I asked my Director of Greek Life,
"What Do You Teach?" He said, "Students."

When I asked my college Literature Professor
"What Do You Teach?" He said, "Literature."
When I asked my Director of Residence Life,
"What Do You Teach?" She said, "Students."

As I grew older and wiser I realized that I got my degree thanks to my professors, but I received my education thanks to my student affairs professionals.

My message to you is simple.
Get To Know Your Student Affairs Professionals.
Even though they are not professors, they are some of the most powerful educators on your campus.
They will help you take your higher education deeper. ★

The Animal School
By Dr. R.H. Reeves

Once upon a time, the animals decided they must do something heroic to meet the problems of "a new world." So they organized a school. They adopted an activity curriculum consisting of running, climbing, swimming and flying. To make it easier to administer the curriculum, all the animals took all the subjects.

The duck was excellent in swimming, in fact better than his instructor, but only made passing grades in flying and was very poor in running. Since he was slow in running, he had to stay after school and also drop swimming in order to practice running. This was kept up until his webbed feet were badly worn and he was only average in swimming. But average was acceptable in school, so nobody worried about that, except the duck.

The rabbit started at the top of the class in running, but she had a nervous breakdown because she had so much make-up work to do in swimming.

The squirrel was excellent in climbing until he developed frustration in flying class where his teacher made him start from the ground up instead of from the treetop down. He also developed a "Charlie horse" from overexertion and then got a C in climbing and a D in running.

The eagle was a problem child and was disciplined severely. In climbing class he beat all the others to the top of the tree, but insisted on using his own way to get there.

At the end of the year, an abnormal eel, that could swim exceedingly well, and also run, climb and fly a little, had the highest grade point average and was named valedictorian.

The prairie dogs stayed out of school and fought the tax levy because the administration would not add digging and burrowing to the curriculum. They apprenticed their children to a badger and later joined the groundhogs and gophers to start a successful private school.

Does this fable have a moral? ★

The Orientation Leader
By Meghan E. Greene

As I woke up at 6 a.m.,
I thought to myself, "Oh, not again!"

My feet hit the floor;
I was soon out the door.

The sun coming up as I began,
Holding my cup of coffee in hand,

To set up my check-in station,
For yet another summer orientation.

I led a small group and performed in a skit.
To the parents, of course, we all were a hit!

Questions! Directions! At once they all come.
It's time for lunch; I should go grab some!

Through the campus, students follow me around.
I begin to count the hours until I can lie down!

Only two more sessions today;
And people actually listen to what I say!

All the work and all the strife;
Has made a difference in someone's life.

This job is so rewarding;
That I can't wait until morning! ★

Parable of The Chinese Bamboo Tree
By Anthony J. D'Angelo

It takes a Chinese Bamboo tree four solid years after planting to finally break ground; Nothing for four years after planting the seed. There is a small bulb which appears eventually, with a little chute coming out of the bulb, but all of the growth during the first four years is underground; Building a deep, fibrous, root structure. On the fifth year the Chinese Bamboo tree grows up to 80 feet! All of the growth is above ground because now it has a massive root structure to support it.

Creating things that have meaning take a very long time. There are no quick fixes in this world. Be patient and persist whether you are creating a campus culture, a company or quality life. ★

Lessons from the Playground
By Daniel E. Ashlock, Jr.

Anyone who knows me can tell you that I often look to themes of childhood when learning or teaching about leadership. Children have an amazing way of looking at things without prejudice. But more importantly, the books children read and the games children play help set up important lessons that can last a lifetime!

Maybe it is the unpretentious creativity of a mindless game. Perhaps it is the uncontrollable laughter of childhood. Or, the inevitable honesty that follows a child around a playground. Whatever the motive, many playground civilities have the ability to teach us how to be better leaders.

Jacks

The game of jacks is simple. Bounce a ball, pick up an increasing number of small, metal "jacks," and then catch the ball before it bounces a second time. The metaphors for leadership are vast with jacks. First, the ball can represent a deadline, a performance, a self-induced pressure or an unpredictable challenge. Before the ball is collected, we too as leaders must collect the resources necessary to finish the job.

The Swings

The repetitive motion of a swing represents, for me, the ongoing duties as leaders must accomplish on a regular basis. Whether it's a treasurer depositing funds in the bank or a secretary sending out thank you notes, every leader has routine tasks to field. Rather than look at these regular duties as chores, think of the swing-set and the soothing feeling of flying to-and-fro. Swinging also gives one time to reflect on the world around them. As a leader, take time to reflect and learn from your own experience.

The Slide

Leaders climb ladders often. Sometimes we climb for the long, smooth ride of a high glider and sometimes we get an unexpected ride on a spiral slide! Today's slides have new variations: tunnels, bumps, turns and textures. Remember to get up at the end of a slide and start on the next slide with eagerness and enthusiasm.

The Monkey Bars

The challenge of a set of monkey bars can be daunting. Some fear the height, others lack the necessary strength. Leaders face many challenges. Like the monkey bars, most of our leadership challenges are conquerable! As a leader, take the time to practice and plan appropriately for your challenges.

Jump Rope

For me, jumping rope is all about stamina. When I reflect on my leadership characteristics, fortitude and stamina are on the top of my list. Finding the proper rhythm for jumping rope is like achieving endurance and resilience as a leader.

Kickball

More important than the rules of kickball is the lesson a child learns in picking the right team. In my opinion, great leaders surround themselves with a team that represents various abilities, strengths and knowledge. Often, the success of the leader is determined by the spirit of the team.

Frisbee

Frisbee is perhaps one of the first lessons we receive about the importance of anticipating the unexpected. Can you recall wild Frisbee tosses on the playground? The Frisbees in our leadership careers can keep us alert on our toes!

Hopscotch

Balance; If you can't learn to balance your life like you had to balance your body in a game of hopscotch, your leadership may be in jeopardy. Take time to work hard, play hard, eat right and to rest when you need.

Tetherball

This was a popular game at my elementary school. Two people battle each other for control of a ball on a rope attached to a pole. Strategy and foresight are as important as strength and endurance in this game. Leaders may find success elusive without goals and action plans.

Tag-You're-It

For me, this childhood game speaks about the importance of interpersonal relationships. The chase is secondary to our need for contact with others. Take time to get to know the people with whom you work.

There are other childhood games from which we can learn— hula-hoop, blowing bubbles, paddle ball, and the teeter-totter among them. I hope you will take time to reminisce about your favorite recess activities and apply them to your life as a student leader! ★

Onward and Upward
By Lucy Shaffer Croft

As a leader, one is often faced with adversity. In August of 1996 life as I had known it changed. That was when my father was diagnosed with advanced melanoma, skin cancer, which eventually spread throughout his body and into his brain. He was my foundation, my spiritual counselor, and my inspiration. He was a man of little material substance but rich in love and heart. Even upon the last month of his life, family and friends would visit him at his house, not to console him, but to listen to his words of wisdom and comfort. I would watch as his frail body mustered up enough energy to share a prayer, a story, a warm smile; simple actions that spoke volumes and touched each visitor with unconditional love.

I remember about two weeks before he passed; he was entertaining a friend for dinner at his small yet cozy home. Her name was Betsy. They were true friends. I would often see them laughing, celebrating or even crying together.

The night they were having dinner, I was playing an indoor soccer game. Normally, I play defense and very rarely score a goal. It was on that particular night where I scored a goal, that I felt inspired to share my news with my father. Upon completion of the game, I quickly said good-bye to my teammates and ran off to visit my father.

When I arrived at his home, Betsy and dad were sitting at the dining room table. My father looked tired and pale; however, I could see by the expression on his face he was enjoying his visit.

"What brings you here, Lulu Belle?" he stated.

"I wanted to share my good news with you daddy," I said. "I scored a goal tonight during our soccer game."

It wasn't a big accomplishment. As a matter fact, it seemed rather trivial compared to surviving a round of chemotherapy or radiation treatment. None-the-same, my father grinned from ear-to-ear. He gave me a big hug full of love and encouragement. No one could hug like my father. It was the kind of hug that rejuvenated you, comforted you and made you feel like you were the most special person on earth.

After sharing my news, I paid my respects and left Betsy and dad to their visit. Little did I know that would be the last night Betsy and my father shared dinner. On April 1, 1994 at 5:40 p.m., my father took his last breath of life with me holding his hand. As quickly as life is given, life is taken away.

At the funeral, I consoled with Betsy who shared a little story with me. She proceeded to tell me that the night I stopped by and shared my news of scoring a goal, my father turned to her after I left and said with great pride, "Bets (as he often called her) I'm going to live another month because Lucy scored a goal–Onward and Upward." Hearing those words, I smiled and knew my life would never be the same.

As a leader, finding good in all things is a special trait. When faced with adversity, rejoice in the simple things, live your life to its fullest. When life gives you lemons, no longer focus on the bitterness but concentrate on the sweetness that you gain from the experience. There are lessons to be learned in every facet of life: "Onward and Upward." ★

The Chipped Tea Cup
By Anthony J. D'Angelo

In preparation for our wedding, my college sweetheart, Christine, and I made an appointment to meet with the priest who would be marrying us. At the meeting we asked Father Greg for advice on how to make our marriage a lifelong and happy spiritual partnership. Much to my surprise, rather than sighting the sometimes out of touch biblical passages that most clergy preached, father Greg told us this simple, yet powerful story.

I know of a beautiful old couple who have been married for over fifty years. When I asked them "What is the key to a happy marriage?"

The older man responded modestly, "Father I don't know exactly the one foundational key, but I will tell you this. Every day Martha and I enjoy sipping tea together in our small sun room. This has become a tradition for us. We have it at the same time and sit in the same seats each day. As a matter of fact, we use the same two cups every single time. One cup has a chip in it and the other does not. The only difference is that when Martha sets the table she gives herself the chipped cup and when I set the table I give it to myself."

Editors Note: Christine & Anthony meet when they were student leaders at West Chester University in Pennsylvania. Christine & Anthony became friends while working together in Student Government. Which shows student leadership experiences not only create bonds of friendship, but also have the potential to create life long bonds of love. ★

The Boy Under The Tree
By David Coleman and Kevin Randall

In the summer recess between freshman and sophomore years in college, I was invited to be an instructor at a high school leadership camp hosted by a college in Michigan. I was already highly involved in most campus activities, and I jumped at the opportunity.

About an hour into the first day of camp, amid the frenzy of icebreakers and forced interactions, I first noticed the boy under the tree. He was a small and skinny, and his obvious discomfort and shyness made him appear frail and fragile. Only fifty feet away, two hundred eager campers were bumping bodies, playing, joking and meeting each other, but the boy under the tree seemed to want to be anywhere other than where he was. The desperate loneliness he radiated almost stopped me from approaching him, but I remembered the instructions from the senior staff to stay alert for campers who might feel left out.

As I walked toward him, I said, "Hi, my name is Kevin, and I'm one of the counselors. It's nice to meet you. How are you?" In a shaky, sheepish voice he reluctantly answered, "Okay, I guess." I calmly asked him if he wanted to join the activities and meet some new people. He quietly replied, "No, this is not really my thing."

I could sense that he was in a new world, that this whole experience was foreign to him. But I somehow knew it wouldn't be right to push him, either. He didn't need a pep talk; he needed a friend. After several silent moments, my first interaction with the boy under the tree was over.

At lunch the next day, I found myself leading camp songs at the top of my lungs for two hundred of my new friends. The campers eagerly participated. My gaze wandered over the mass of noise and movement and was caught by the image of the boy from under the tree, sitting alone, staring out the window. I nearly forgot the words to the song I was supposed to be leading.

At my first opportunity, I tried again, with the same questions as before: "How are you doing? Are you okay?" To which he again replied, "Yeah, I'm all right. I just don't really get into this stuff." As I left the cafeteria, I realized this was going to take more time and effort than I had thought— if it was even possible to get through to him at all.

That evening at our nightly staff meeting, I made my concerns about him known. I explained to my fellow staff members my impression of him and asked them to pay special attention and spend time with him when they could.

The days I spend at camp each year fly by faster than any others I have known. Thus, before I know it, mid-week had dissolved into the final night of camp, and I was chaperoning the "last dance." The students were doing all they could to savor every last moment with their new "best friends" — friends they would probably never see again.

As I watched the campers share their parting moments I suddenly saw what would be one of the most vivid memories of my life. The boy from under the tree, who had stared blankly out the kitchen window, was now a shirtless dancing wonder. He owned the dance floor as he and two girls proceeded to cut a rug. I watched as he shared meaningful, intimate time with people at whom he couldn't even look just days earlier. I couldn't believe it was the same person.

In October of my sophomore year, a late-night phone call pulled me away from my chemistry book. A soft spoken, unfamiliar voice asked politely, "Is Kevin there?"

"You're talking to him. Who's this?"

"This is Tommy Johnson's mom. Do you remember Tommy from leadership camp?"

The boy under the tree. How could I not remember?

"Yes, I do," I said. "He's a very nice young man. How is he?"

An abnormally long pause followed, the Mrs. Johnson said, "My Tommy was walking home from school this week when he was hit by a car and killed." Shocked I offered my condolences.

"I just wanted to call you," she said, "because Tommy mentioned you so many times. I wanted you to know that he went back to school this fall with confidence. He made new friends.

His grades went up. And even went out on a few dates. I just wanted to thank you for making a difference for Tommy. The last few months were the best few months of his life."

In that instant, I realized how easy it is to give a bit of yourself every day. You may never know how much each gesture may mean to someone else. I tell this story as often as I can, and when I do, I urge others to look out for their own "boy under the tree." ★

"Live Your Life
So That Your Children
Can Tell Their Children
That You Not Only
Stood For Something—
You Acted On It!"

Anthony J. D'Angelo

We Want Your Story For Volume II !

WOULD YOU LIKE TO SEE YOUR STORY IN INSPIRATION FOR STUDENT LEADERS™ VOLUME II?

All of the stories that you have read in this book were submitted student leaders like you. We would love to have you contribute a story, poem, quote or cartoon to:

Inspiration for Student Leaders™ Volume II

Even though we are planning to launch several other Inspiration Books over the next few years, (see inside front cover for details) we are always looking for more Student Leader Stories to create Volume II.

Feel free to send us stories you write yourself. It also could be a favorite poem, quotation, cartoon or story you have seen that speaks to your Student Leadership Experience. Just make sure to send as much information about you and the source of your submission.

Please send your submissions to:
The Collegiate EmPowerment Company, Inc.
The Inspiration Book Series™ Submission Department
Email It To: Inspiration@Collegiate-EmPowerment.com

If your submission is accepted & approved your message will touch the lives of thousands of Student Leaders across the country! (Of course you'll get a free book too!)

Permissions and Trademarks

We would like to thank all the contributing authors
for their permission to reprint their submissions.

What Every College Creed Ought To Be ©1995 Anthony J. D'Angelo
Do It Anyway ©2001 Elizabeth Randazzese
True Leaders Never Lose ©2001 David Tukey
The Day I Was A Dipstick ©1998 Anthony J. D'Angelo
The Quandary of Jewels ©2002 Daniel E. Ashlock
Getting An Education, Not Just A Degree ©1998 Anthony J. D'Angelo
Women Who Dare & Who Helped Us All ©2001 Anthony J. D'Angelo
Complications ©1999 Mark Walker
The Purpose of Student Leaders ©2001 Elizabeth Randazzese
The Chopsticks of Heaven & Hell ©1998 Anthony J. D'Angelo
Lessons From A Fly ©2001By:Dan Oltersdorf
Just Because It's Tradition, Doesn't Make It Right ©1995 Anthony J. D'Angelo
Leadership Demonstrated By Picking Up Trash ©2001 George Brelsford
How To Get An A On Your Final Exam ©1995 Anthony J. D'Angelo
Pebbles In Your Pockets ©2001 Thomas W. Smith
The Secret to Leadership ©2001 Elizabeth Randazzese
What Legacy Will You Leave? ©1998 Anthony J. D'Angelo
What Is A Leader? ©2001 Stephen M. Vindigni
A Simple Lesson About Leadership ©1996 Anthony J. D'Angelo
Seeking To Understand ©2000 Brian Dassler
If You Talk The Talk, You Better Walk The Walk ©1996 By Anthony J. D'Angelo
What Being A Student Leader Is All About ©1998 Anthony J. D'Angelo
There Are Professors and Then There Are Educators ©1998 Anthony J. D'Angelo
The Orientation Leader ©2001 Meghan Greene
The Parable of The Chinese Bamboo Tree ©1997 By Anthony J. D'Angelo
Lessons From The Playground ©2002 Dan Ashlock
Onward and Upward ©2002 Lucy Croft
The Chipped Tea Cup ©1998 Anthony J. D'Angelo
The Boy Under The Tree ©1998 By David Coleman and Kevin Randall

Please note the stories that are public domain or were written by both unknown and anonymous authors are not included. We have exercised due diligence but have been unable to locate copyright holders of these stories. If you have any information concerning the copyrights of these stories, please contact The Collegiate EmPowerment Company, Inc.

For your consideration please note the following trademark references contained within this work:

Chicken Soup For The Soul® is a trademark of Chicken Soup for The Soul Enterprises and is used for identification purposes only.

The Strategic Coach® is a trademark of The Strategic Coach, Inc. and is used for identification purposes only.

The following are trademarks of The Collegiate EmPowerment Company, Inc.: The Inspiration Book Series™ and all series related titles including but not limited to: Inspiration For Resident Assistants™, Inspiration For Greeks™, Inspiration For Student Leaders™, Inspiration For LGBT Students & Their Allies, Inspiration For Student Athletes™, Inspiration For Student Affairs Professionals™ and Inspiration for International Students™.

Additional trademarks include: EmPower X!™, Getting An Education, Not Just A Degree™, You Can't Lead Others Until You First Lead Yourself™, Taking Higher Education Deeper™ and Helping You Take Higher Education Deeper™, Don't Major In Minor Things™.

What College Forgets To Teach You® is a registered trademark of The Collegiate EmPowerment Company, Inc.. This mark extends to all seminar titles expressed in this document under the domain of The What College Forgets To Teach You® Seminar Series.

For more information regarding the use or license of the The Collegiate EmPowerment Company, Inc. trademarks please contact 1.877.338.8246.

Every Great Idea Has A Story Behind It...
The Story of The Collegiate EmPowerment Company.

Higher education in the United States of America is one of the fastest growing sectors in the US economy. This expansion is occurring at an unprecedented rate in which enrollment is predicted to exceed the 16 million mark by the year 2007. In fact the United Nations reports that world demand for higher education is now over 75 million people. Institutions of higher education exist in small towns and in big cities, in every state, province and country.

"1 Out of Every 6 College Students Will Drop Out"

But the United States serves as a painful reminder of reality. Of the over 1.6 million new students who enroll in college each year, 1 out of every 6 will drop out within the first 6 months of enrollment. This equates into a stunning attrition rate of 33%. (Source: US Department of Education)

Since 1995 The Collegiate EmPowerment Company (CEC) has been on the front lines assisting universities in combating this pervasive challenge. As a pioneer in personal empowerment education for college students, The CEC is the nation's leader of high impact seminars, customized coaching and innovative empowerment resources, exclusively designed to serve both universities and college students alike.

The seeds of the organization were planted in the early 1990's by founder Anthony J. D'Angelo. As an undergraduate in Health Promotion at West Chester University (PA), Anthony created the prototype template for The CEC, via his senior thesis project, WellnessWorks. The organizational plan received an A+ from his spring semester professor. Yet during his 1994 summer internship in which the plan was implemented, D'Angelo received a C from his academic supervisor. The justification for the C grade on the project was purported to be due to the project's "incompletion." Despite the C, D'Angelo carried on with his vision and never looked back. He focused on progress, not perfection.

In the spring of 1995 after 6 months of graduating college, Anthony was inspired to take action on his vision. At the young age of 23, he left his cushy job, liquidated his personal savings, got a "grant" from his Discover Card (he went into over $150,000 in personal debt to fund the organization) and drove across the Mid-Atlantic to interview over 5,000 college students and 1,000 university professionals to gain the pulse of what college students were missing. Six months into his journey he found it.

When ask what he discovered, Anthony states, "Based on my first hand interviews, I began to see quite a sad reality of the average college student in America. What I came comprehend was that for most students, college has become an oppressive existence; One which I would call 'The killing field of the human soul'".

However bold this statement may be, it is a fundamental fact that most college students today have absolutely no idea why they are in college. Aside from the American Social contract which assumes college is the next step after high school for any "right minded" young adult.

"Most College Students Get A Degree, But Not An Education."

"Sadly enough most college students today go to college and get a degree, but not an education," says D'Angelo. "We help college students get an education by showing them what college forgets to teach them. It is our vision to take higher education deeper."

Taking Higher Education Deeper™ is not only the mantra of The Collegiate EmPowerment Company, it has become the mission. Having served over 1 Million college students and 2,500 professionals from over 1,500 campuses across North America, the firm continues create a new model of deeper education for the 21st Century.

When asked "What is the long term vision for The Collegiate EmPowerment Company?" D'Angelo states, "We are creating a new kind of "school" for a new kind of world. After all, the world as we know it is less then 15 years old. For in 1989 the Berlin Wall came down and in 1995 the World Wide Web went up. It is a completely new world for us all. With this new world, come new challenges. With these new challenges, come new ways of educating people for the future and it is our every intention to be at the fore front of this educational revolution. The 20th Century was about Content, but the 21st Century is about Context. The majority of educational institutions in the United States are still focus on the Content— the curriculum. The Collegiate EmPowerment Company is here to help institutions expand their Context by Helping Them Take Higher Education Deeper."

The Overview Of The
Collegiate EmPowerment Company, Inc.

The Collegiate EmPowerment Company, Inc.

"Helping You Take Higher Education Deeper™"

The Collegiate EmPowerment Company is a nationally recognized educational firm exclusively dedicated to serving highly motivated college students and professional educators within the community of Higher Education. We empower collegiate students & professionals alike via our:

- Collegiate EmPowerment Coaching Services for Professionals
- Collegiate EmPowerment Seminars for Students
- Collegiate EmPowerment Products & Resources

Since 1995, we have empowered over 1 million college students and over 2,500 professionals from over 1,500 college campuses via the following Collegiate EmPowerment Product & Service formats:

The Inspiration Book Series™ is a one of a kind book series written By College Students For College Students. This seven part series is a compilation of real life stories of Encouragement, Humor and Motivation by College Students For College Students. The series titles include Inspiration for: Resident Assistants, Greeks, Student Leaders, LGBT Students & Their Allies, College Students, Student Affairs Professionals and International Students. One dollar of every book sold is donated to a National Association which serves the specific student group.

"Young Adults EmPowering Young Adults"

EmPower X! is the instructional team of The Collegiate EmPowerment Company. EmPower X! is an elite team of young, passionate & professional adults, all under the age of 30, who facilitate the Get A Life ... Outside The Classroom Seminar Series™. Each member of EmPower X! is a Certified EmPower X! Coach™, who has been hand selected & personally trained by Anthony J. D'Angelo and The EmPower X! Casting Team. High energy & inspiration by young adults for young adults is the trademark of EmPower X!

The cornerstone of the Collegiate EmPowerment Company is our Get A Life Outside The Classroom™ Seminar Series. A curriculum series of over 30 comprehensive & integrated seminars, created by Anthony D'Angelo and The CEC Seminar Design Team, exclusively designed to address the challenges typical of most college students. The series consists of four different levels of seminars, each containing distinct concepts, tools, strategies and systems. Each seminar reinforces the others and deepens a student's understanding of his or her own vision & values. Every seminar module is an informative, interactive and inspiring experience coached by a member of EmPower X!

The Collegiate EmPowerment Advantage is a uniquely customized coaching experience for highly committed student affairs professionals and professional educators. The experience consists of a series of monthly coaching sessions and quarterly on site workshops. The program is four years in duration, with participants committing to one year at a time. The Collegiate EmPowerment Advantage is the first lifetime focusing school designed exclusively for professionals who want to take Higher Education Deeper. Within this school there is a constant focus on uniqueness, on enabling each participant to identify his or her Core Genius and then transform it into endless empowerment on a campus community. Participants of the experience benefit in four ways: 1) Increased Peace Time, 2) Increased Professional Productivity, 3) Increased Clarity & Balance, and 4) Increased Simplicity

Our Vision:

Our Vision Is To Help You Take Higher Education Deeper.

Our Mission:

We Help You Take Higher Education Deeper in three simple yet powerful ways:

1. We Teach Students How To Get An Education and Not Just A Degree.
2. We EmPower Professionals So They In Turn Can Help Students.
3. We Outfit Higher Education with Collegiate EmPowerment Tools.

We are an educational firm dedicated to serving highly motivated college students and dedicated professionals within the community of Higher Education with the most interactive, inspiring and informative seminars, products and services. We empower collegiate students & professionals alike via our:

- Collegiate EmPowerment Seminars for Students
  - EmPower X!- Our seminar coaching team of young adults
  - The Get A Life… Outside of The Classroom Seminar Series™
- Collegiate EmPowerment Coaching Services for Professionals
  - The Collegiate EmPowerment Advantage
- Collegiate EmPowerment Products for both students & professionals
  - The Inspiration Book Series
  - The Collegiate EmPowerment Tools

Our Code Of Conduct:

1. We Are Here To Serve You.
2. We Are Passionate & Professional
3. We Show Up On Time.
4. We Do What We Say We Are Going To Do.
5. We Say Please and We Say Thank You.

What Makes Us So Fundamentally Different?

1. We are not a speaker's agency.
   We are an educational firm.
2. We are not motivational speakers.
   We are Collegiate EmPowerment Coaches.
3. We are not trainers.
   We are Coaches. Training is for animals.
   Coaching is for people.
4. We are not about one shot "talks, speeches or lectures"
   We have a comprehensive 4 year curriculum with over 100 seminar modules.
5. We are not interested in working with just anyone.
   We only serve highly motivated students & professionals within Higher Education.
6. We are not going anywhere.
   We only get better and better, year after year and we won't stop.

"Young Adults EmPowering Young Adults"

The mission of EmPower X! is to Awaken, Enliven, Inspire and Empower young adults to significantly enhance their quality of life in order to achieve and fulfill worthwhile purposes in the world. We meet this noble challenge via our EmPower X! Seminar Experiences which are help on college campuses. We first help young adults to discover, nurture and apply their own Personal Leadership. Secondly we introduce them to the concepts, tools and resources of personal empowerment education. This synergistic approach allows us to help young adults become more by supporting the never ending search for the best within themselves.

Every young person is an X.
For some young people, that X means being an unknown.
For a few like you, that X means being a multiplication factor.
You are different. You are a leader. You make things happen.
While most of your peers are merely getting a degree, you are getting an education.
We help people like you take your higher education deeper.

Life is short. You have dreams.
We realize this and make it our mission
to help you achieve those dreams.
We are a team of dream architects. Some people design buildings.
We help people like you design you life.
See you on your campus soon!

What Makes EmPower X! So Cooly Unique?

* We were started by young adults for young adults with young adults in mind
* We are the only team of young adults dedicated to empowering other young adults
* We have over 35 seminar modules to choose from and they're all for young adults
* We offer multiple visits to your campus which allows students to benefit exponentially
* All of our seminars are fun, high-energy and interactive, multimedia experiences
* All of our seminars synergize with each other which offers a residual impact
* All of our seminars are memorable experiences for your campus community
* All of our seminars are developed by young adults for young adults
* All of our coaches are young adults under the age of 30
* All of our seminars are backed by a 100% money back guarantee
* If you and your students don't like it, you don't pay for it

Pretty cool, wouldn't you say?

The Inspiration Book Series

An Overview of Get a Life...Outside The Classroom!

The Collegiate EmPowerment Company is an educational firm dedicated to coaching college students who are looking to create a balanced and meaningful life. Sadly enough, most college students go to college and get a degree, but not an education. We are dedicated to serving Student Affairs Professionals and Student Leaders like yourself by Helping You Take Higher Education Deeper. We are your partner in assisting today's college students in getting an education while they pursue their degree. We at the Collegiate EmPowerment Company achieve this goal through our *Get A Life... Outside of The Classroom!*® Seminar Series. This seminar series is the most comprehensive personal development curriculum ever designed for young adults aged 18–28. Students who participate in the seminars will benefit in the following ways:

- **Greater Levels of Self Confidence** about their personal and professional capabilities
- The application and development of **Personal Leadership**
- **Increased Sense of Clarity** regarding one's life and its direction for the future
- Increased abilities for **Cultivating Diversity and Creating Community**
- **Greater Happiness**
- The development of a **Deeper Meaning and Sense of Purpose and Contribution**
- **Dramatic Improvement in Relationships,** both personal and professional
- The development of **Organizational Leadership Skills**
- **Expanded Awareness of Life**
- The development of a **Balanced Life**; in the areas of emotional EmPowerment, intellectual EmPowerment, physical EmPowerment, spiritual EmPowerment, time EmPowerment, relationship EmPowerment, professional EmPowerment and financial EmPowerment

The Four Levels of The *Get A Life... Outside of The Classroom* Series:

Level I: Campus EmPowerment Advantage
Taking Higher Education Deeper

Level II: Personal Leadership Advantage
You Can't Lead Others Until You First Lead Yourself

Level III: Personal EmPowerment Advantage
Our Version of The Wellness Model on Steroids

Level IV: The Student Leader EmPowerment Advantage
Why Most Student Organizations Don't Work and What to Do About It

The Get A Life...Outside The Classroom
Seminar Series Overview

Taking Higher Education Deeper™
Level I: General Student Seminars
The introductory level of the Get A Life... Outside The Classroom™ Seminar Series, these seminars are perfect for campus community events such as Orientation, Convocation, Alcohol Awareness Week and Commencement.

Reflections On The College Blue Book
Get A Life...Outside of The Classroom (Freshman Orientation)
Getting An Education, Not Just A Degree™
What The Classroom Forgets To Teach You (Freshman Orientation)
How To Maximize Your BUZZ!™
What The Classroom Forgets To Teach You About Alcohol (Campus Community)
Taking Higher Education Deeper™
What The Classroom Forgets To Teach You About 21st Century Education (Campus Community)
How To Get Out Of Credit Card Debt Before You Graduate™
What The Classroom Forgets To Teach You About Credit Cards (Campus Community)
Lessons Learned From College
What The Classroom Forgets To Teach You About Graduation (Commencement)

Getting An Education Not Just A Degree™
Level II: Student Involvement Seminars
The perfect level to help you meet your programming needs for Athletes, Greeks, RAs and Student Leadership Conferences. All coaches who coach theses seminars have first hand personal experience to relate to your specific student group.

The Mindset Of A Champion™
What The Classroom Forgets To Teach You About Being An Athlete
What Animal House Never Taught Me™
What The Classroom Forgets To Teach You About Being Greek
What You Do Makes A Powerful Difference Around Here™
What The Classroom Forgets To Teach You About Student Activities
It's Not Just A Job It's A Lifestyle™
What The Classroom Forgets To Teach You About Being A Resident Assistant
The Student Government Myth: Leadership Is Not About Holding A Position. It's About Having A Passion™
What The Classroom Forgets To Teach You About Student Government
Why Most Student Organizations Don't Work & What To Do About It™
What The Classroom Forgets To Teach You About Being A Student Leader

The Get A Life…Outside The Classroom Seminar Series Overview

You Can't Lead Others Until You First Lead Yourself™
Level III: Personal Leadership Seminars
This level is the core foundation of Get A Life… Outside The Classroom™ Seminar Series. At this level we unlock the foundation key to lifetime fulfillment and achievement: Personal Leadership. The concept of Personal Leadership serves as a tool box containing 7 tools which when applied generate a specific source of Personal EmPowerment.

The Seven Tools Of Personal Leadership Are:
1. Vision: The Source of Unending EmPowerment
2. X-Think: The Source of Exponential EmPowerment
3. Action: The Source of Unlimited EmPowerment
4. Belief: The Source of Unshakable EmPowerment
5. Principles: The Source of Uncompromising EmPowerment
6. TeamThink: The Source of Untied EmPowerment
7. Faith: The Source of Ultimate EmPowerment

Each tool has its own seminar module which shows the student how to discover,apply and utilize the tool in everyday life.

Within each session, participants are taught:
*   The 7 Benefits Of The Tool
*   The 7 Concepts Underlying The Tool
*   The 7 Application Strategies of Implementing The Tool

Below is a listing of the Personal Leadership Seminar Modules:
You Can't Lead Others Until You First Lead Yourself ™
What The Classroom Forgets To Teach You About Personal Leadership
Most People Die When They're 27, But They're Not Buried Until They're 77!™
What The Classroom Forgets To Teach You About Personal Vision
Are You An Unknown Or Are You An Multiplication Factor™
What The Classroom Forgets To Teach You About X-Think
The Difference One Person Can Make™
What The Classroom Forgets To Teach You About Personal Action
Success Leaves Clues™
What The Classroom Forgets To Teach You About Proven Principles
If You Think You Can Or You Think You Can't, Either Way You're Right™
What The Classroom Forgets To Teach You About Personal Beliefs
(The Karate Board Breakthrough)
You Can't Become A Somebody Without The Help Of Someone™
What The Classroom Forgets To Teach You About TeamThink
There Is More To You Than You Think™
What The Classroom Forgets To Teach You About Faith

The Get A Life…Outside The Classroom Seminar Series Overview

Don't Major In Minor Things™

Level IV: Personal EmPowerment Seminars

The fourth level of The Get A Life… Outside of The Classroom™ Seminar Series is Personal EmPowerment. This is The CEC's version of the "Wellness Model On Steroids". We have taken the traditional wellness model and kicked it up a notch. It is now the most comprehensive and synergistic EmPowerment System for young adults. Each seminar module highlights the seven most powerful principles which the CEC Seminar Development Team has uncovered from the latest cutting edge human potential research. These seven core principles have been engineered into the CEC's EmPowerment Transformation Model to create a powerful seminar experience for students.

The seminars cover the following eight dimensions:

The Internal Dimensions:	The External Dimensions:
Physical EmPowerment	Time EmPowerment
Emotional EmPowerment	Relationship EmPowerment
Intellectual EmPowerment	Professional EmPowerment
Spiritual EmPowerment	Financial EmPowerment

Below is a listing of the Personal EmPowerment Seminar Modules:

The Grass On The Other Side Is Whatever Color You Make It™
What The Classroom Forgets To Teach You About Emotional EmPowerment

How To Become A Kick-Ass Intellectual Powerhouse!™
What The Classroom Forgets To Teach You About Intellectual EmPowerment

How To Get Naturally Wired & Unleash You Natural Storehouse of Crack!™
What The Classroom Forgets To Teach You About Physical EmPowerment

You Are Not A Human Being Going Through A Spiritual Experience,
You Are A Spiritual Being Going Through A Human Experience.™
What The Classroom Forgets To Teach You About Spiritual EmPowerment

Creating The Time Of Your Life™
What The Classroom Forgets To Teach You About Time EmPowerment

Men Are Like Microwaves & Women Are Like Crockpots™
What The Classroom Forgets To Teach You About Relationships

You, Inc.: You Are The President Of Your Own
Professional Services Company™
What The Classroom Forgets To Teach You About Professional EmPowerment

Plan To Be A Millionaire?™
What The Classroom Forgets To Teach You About Financial EmPowerment

-------- THE -------
STUDENT LEADER
EMPOWERMENT ADVANTAGE™

The Student Leader EmPowerment Advantage is a revolutionary model of student leadership development. From our experience of working with over 1 million college students from over 1,500 college campuses we have learned:

Leadership Development Is Like Taking A Shower;
If you only do it once a year, You Will Stink!™

The Collegiate EmPowerment Company has created this new format of training, to help you help your student leaders. The Student Leader EmPowerment Advantage™ is a four part seminar experience consisting of 4 separate one day EmPowershops™ (workshops) over the semester or academic year.

EmPowershop I: The Compelling Vision Cultivator™
Core Focus: Creating Your Organization's Strategic Plan
This kickoff session occurs at the start of the academic semester. In this session student leaders identify their organization's goals and create the operating framework for the upcoming year.

EmPowershop II: The Team Synergy Creator™
Core Focus: Teamwork & Delegation
In this session student leaders receive their own customized Leadership & Core Genius Profiler™. In the second half of this session, participants create a Team Synergy Delegation Plan™ for their organization.

EmPowershop III: The Core Process Captivator™
Core Focus: Documenting Organizational Processes & Systems
The third session is crucial to long term organizational success. In this session leaders capture what they have done during their tenure so they can empower future leaders.

EmPowershop IV: The Torch Passing Catalyst™
Core Focus: EmPowering The Next Generation of Leaders
Each participant brings one member of their organization to this final session, which occurs during the end of the semester. Together the students plan for their organization's future. The session concludes with a powerful Torch Passing Experience™

Only highly motivated and committed student leaders are applicable. This program is not for everyone and students looking for a quick fix need not apply. A school selects 25 student leaders from various student organizations to partake in this in depth and transformational experience. Each one day EmPowershop takes place from 10 am to 5 pm on your campus. The enrollment fee for The Student Leader EmPowerment Advantage™ is $12,000 inclusive. Advance payment is required to partake in this truly revolutionary one of a kind experience.

PLEASE ASK YOUR SEMINAR CONSULTANT FOR MORE DETAILS
For more information call toll free: 1-877-EDUTAIN
(338-8246)

The Collegiate EmPowerment Company
Seminar & Service Formats

The Collegiate EmPowerment Company offers a wide range of seminar and service formats to meet both your event needs as well as your budget. Seminar times range from as short as a 45 minute keynote to our four one day retreats which occur 4 times over an academic year. Our seminar & service formats are as follows:

- 2 hours (our standard format)
- 1 day format (keynote, 2 workshops and a wrap-up session)
- The Frequent EmPowerment Service: 2 or 3 two hour seminars spaced over a semester
- The Student Leader EmPowerment Advantage: 4 one day sessions over a semester
- The Collegiate EmPowerment Advantage (one-to-one): 1 year of monthly coaching
- The Collegiate EmPowerment Advantage (package):
  1 year of coaching + 1 on site seminar
- The Collegiate EmPowerment Advantage (one site):
  1 year of coaching + 4 quarterly sessions

One of the most powerful and optimal formats to utilize is our cutting edge Frequent EmPowerment Service. This service provides you and your students with multiple campus visits per semester, first priority bookings and discounts on EmPowerment Products. (Please speak with a CEC Seminar Consultant for more information about the Frequent EmPowerment Service.)

Another added feature of working with The Collegiate EmPowerment Company is our multiple coaching staff. You can choose from a wide range of coaching options. For keynotes and 2 hour seminars we recommend the use of one instructor. If you are planning a day long event we recommend using 2 instructors. In the case of full day leadership conferences we suggest that you allow the CEC to assist you in coordinating the entire event.

In addition to having multiple coaching options, The Collegiate EmPowerment Company offers 3 different coach levels to best serve your campus as well as your budget. The three distinct coaching levels are as follows:

Level I: EmPower X! Associate Level Coach
Level II: EmPower X! Senior Level Coach
Level III: A Master Level Collegiate EmPowerment Coach

The Level I & II Coaches comprise our EmPower X! Team. Each coach is fully certified to conduct EmPower X! Seminar Experiences. The primary difference between an Associate Level Coach and a Senior Level Coach is the number of seminars which he/she has conducted. An Associate Level Coach becomes a Senior Level Coach upon the completion of 50 or more seminar presentations. This distinction is reflected in service fee for each level.

A Master Level Collegiate EmPowerment Coach is a professional educator who is a certified Collegiate EmPowerment Coach. This certification process is an apprenticeship consisting of over 4,000 hours of intensive Collegiate EmPowerment immersion. The apprenticeship is a four year transformative process. Upon completion of this experience the coach gains full mastery of all Collegiate EmPowerment Seminars & Services.

The Enrollment & Service Fees*:

45 MIN KEYNOTE & 2 HR SEMINAR RATE

Coach Level	Service Fee	Day Rate
EmPower X! Associate Level Coach	$1,500 All Inclusive	NA
EmPower X! Senior Level Coach	$2,500 All Inclusive	$3,500 Inc.
Master Level Coach	$4,000 All Inclusive	$5,000 Inc.

THE FREQUENT EMPOWERMENT SERVICE*

Format	Service Fee	Price Per Seminar
2 Two Hour Seminars	$3,000 All Inclusive	Only $1,500
3 Two Hour Seminars	$6,000 All Inclusive	Only $2,000

This service is limited to institutions within a 200 mile radius of The Lehigh Valley Area, PA.

THE STUDENT LEADER EMPOWERMENT ADVANTAGE™

Format	Service Fee	Price Per Seminar
4 Complete One Day Seminars	$12,000 All Inclusive	Only $3,000 Per 1 day seminar!

THE COLLEGIATE EMPOWERMENT ADVANTAGE™
A Coaching Service for Student Affairs Professionals:

Format	Enrollment Fee	Number of Participants
1 Year of Monthly Tele-Coaching	$3,500	1 Professional
1 Year of Monthly Tele-Coaching + 1 Campus Visit	$6,500 Inclusive	1 Professional Campus Community
4 Quarterly Onsite Sessions + Monthly Tele-Coaching	$15,000 Inclusive	10 Mid-Level Professionals
4 Quarterly Onsite Sessions + Monthly Tele-Coaching	$25,000	Inclusive 25 Mid to Upper Level Professionals

Due to the uniquely client centric and customized service of The Collegiate EmPowerment Company, payment in full is required upon contract for enrollment in all seminars & coaching services.

Please note enrollment & service fees are subject to change.

 **The Book That Started It All!** This collection of over 50 stories from actual RAs on the front lines will help you to renew your vision of what it means to be a RA. Learn from others about the challenges, fun times and rewards which come from serving students. One dollar of every book sold is donated to ACUHO-I. The perfect tool for RA training!

"This book offers an encouraging & inspirational message that will keep any RA motivated to make a difference!"
Joe Patane, from MTV's Real World Miami & former Resident Director at UC Berkeley.

 **You Can't Lead Others Until You First Lead Yourself!** This collection of stories and reflections will help you remember leadership is about having a passion and not just a position. One dollar of every book sold is donated NACA. Makes a great gift for your organization's members as well as your student leaders!

"These inspiring stories will undoubtedly be an important source of support for college student leaders."
Alan B. Davis, Executive Director of The National Association for Campus Activities (NACA)

 **What Animal House Forgot To Teach You!** This book will help you understand the true meaning of being a fraternity man and a sorority woman as you honor the unbreakable bonds of sisterhood and brotherhood. One dollar of every book sold is donated to AFA. The perfect resource for every chapter house library!

"This book will touch and nurture the soul of any Fraternity Man or Sorority Woman who reads it!"
Mark Victor Hansen, Co-Author of the #1 NY Times Bestselling Chicken Soup for The Soul® Series

 **Success Is The Freedom To Be Yourself!** Discover the Encouragement to be who you are, the Empowerment to transform negativity and the Motivation to life your life as you want in this compilation of stories from LGBT Students and their allies. One dollar of every book sold is donated to The National Consortium of Directors of LGBT Resources in Higher Education. This book should be on the bookshelf of every educator, student and ally!

"Thank goodness for this book. It's going to save some very important lives."
Kate Bornstein, Author of Gender Outlaw and My Gender Workbook.

The Inspiration Book Series

LOOKING FOR THE PERFECT WAY TO INSPIRE YOURSELF & YOUR STUDENTS?

Inspiration™
THE BOOK SERIES — Inspiration Books make great gifts for your students and members. The perfect way to say Thank You, Congratulations, Welcome or Job Well Done!

ORDER IN ANY COMBINATION & SAVE MONEY!

All major credit cards and purchase orders accepted.

Number of Books	Approximate Discount Rate	Price Per Book	Bulk Rate Price	Shipping & Handling	Total Price	You Save
1-9	NA	$14.95	NA	$2.00/each	$16.95	NA
10	10%	$13.45	$134.50	$15	$157.50	$15.00
25	15%	$12.70	$317.50	$20	$337.50	$56.25
50	20%	$12.00	$600.00	$25	$625.00	$147.50
75	25%	$11.25	$843.75	$30	$873.75	$277.50
100	30%	$10.50	$1050.00	$40	$1090.00	$445.00
150	35%	$9.75	$1462.50	$50	$1512.50	$780.00
200	40%	$9.00	$1800.00	$60	$1860.00	$1190.00

For Bulk Discount Orders Please Contact
The Collegiate EmPowerment Company, Inc.
Email: Info@Collegiate-EmPowerment.com
Toll free at: 1-877-EDUTATIN (338-8246)
Or visit www.Collegiate-EmPowerment.com